RECIPES
from the
OLD MILL

RECIPES
from the
OLD MILL

BAKING with
WHOLE GRAINS

Sarah E. Myers
and Mary Beth Lind

Illustrations by Elizabeth Anthony

Good 🌳 Books®

Intercourse, PA 17534

ACKNOWLEDGEMENT

The recipes "Roberta's Sourdough Rye," "Manuel's Rye Sour," and "Hot Cross Buns" are from THE LAUREL'S KITCHEN BREAD BOOK by Laurel Robertson, with Carol Flinders and Bronwen Godfrey. Copyright © 1984 by The Blue Mountain Center of Meditation, Inc. Reprinted by permission of Random House, Inc.

Design by Dawn J. Ranck

RECIPES FROM THE OLD MILL
Copyright © 1995 by Sarah E. Myers and Mary Beth Lind

Good Books, Intercourse, PA 17534
International Standard Book Number: 1-56148-176-9
Library of Congress Catalog Card Number: 95-35567

Library of Congress Cataloging-in-Publication Data

Myers, Sarah E.
     Recipes from the old mill : baking with whole grains / Sarah E. Myers and Mary Beth Lind.
          p. cm.
     Includes index.
     ISBN 1-56148-176-9
     1. Baking. 2. Cookery (Cereals) I. Lind, Mary Beth. II. Title.
TX765.M94   1995
641.8'15--dc20

95-35567
CIP

Table of Contents

Tips

INTRODUCTION

In 1954, when our father, a country doctor, bought land on which he wished to build his medical clinic, an old building sat at one end of the acreage, and a stream flowed through the property. This old building and this stream were a water-powered grist mill and a mill stream.

We spent many happy hours boating on the mill pond in summer and ice skating on the mill pond in the winter. Inside the old building, the smells of wood, water, and flour blended into an incense which seemed timeless. It was a wonderful place to sit—feeling the throb of the mill stones rhythmically turning, hearing the water rushing into the turbine, and seeing the grain entering the hopper only to reappear as flour. Somehow, that hard, dry, whole grain was turned into a fine, soft flour.

When our uncle, the miller, wasn't looking, we would slide our hands quickly under the spout and grab a handful of flour, quietly stuffing it into our mouths. Then sputtering as we choked on the dry flour, we were chased away, temporarily. I say temporarily, because there was something about that timeless smell of wood, water, and flour that drew us back.

And so, years later, we are drawn back to this old mill. As adults we no longer steal fresh ground flour from the spout and savor it in our mouths; instead we grind the grains and bake fresh breads which we savor and share.

This heritage and joy of fresh whole grains and baking is what we would like to share with you.

—Sarah E. Myers
and Mary Beth Lind

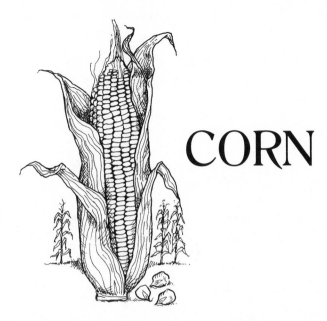

CORN

Corn originated in the Americas. In fact, most early American civilizations were based on it. The Aztec and Mayan cultures of Central and South America, as well as the Appalachian Seneca Indian culture in West Virginia, were all corn cultures. While our present day diet is not based on any one grain, the grain most often raised in this part of Appalachia is corn. At our mill most of what we custom-grind is corn.

Not all corn is alike. There is flint or dent corn, open pollinated or hybrid, yellow or white, field corn or sweet corn. When grinding corn for cornmeal, we most often use a yellow, field, dent, hybrid corn. Yellow is most common and best liked locally. However, if you live further south, you probably prefer white corn. The difference between the two is mostly skin-deep. Yellow corn does contain more Vitamin A than white corn.

The corn most commonly ground is field corn. It is usually dried well, which enhances its grinding and keeping quality. (If you have trouble with your cornmeal molding, either the corn was not dried properly before it was ground, or you are storing it improperly.)

Most often, field corn is a dent corn. The name comes from the dent that forms at the top of the kernel when the corn is dried. Each kernel is composed of both hard and soft starches. When ground, these starches yield the characteristic cornmeal texture.

Flint corn, the alternate of dent corn, is better known as Indian corn. Its kernels contain soft starch in the center with a coating of flint-hard starch all around it. When flint corn is ground, it makes a corn flour instead of a cornmeal. However, the flour is rougher than wheat flour because of the flint-hard starch surrounding the kernel. Corn flour or cornmeal, unlike wheat flour, contains no gluten and so cannot be used alone when you bake with yeast.

Unfortunately, most of the corn available on the market is hybrid. While that means crop yields are greater, it also means that some of the versatility and quality of open pollinated, traditional corns are lost. Traditionally, a farmer saved some of the best kernels for next year's seed; thus, one never needed to buy corn seed. This seed was highly prized, and each area or family had its favorite variety. In our area, one of the favorites was "Bloody Butcher corn." It made a delicious cornmeal.

At our mill, when a farmer brings corn to be ground, we accept toll or cash payment. Toll is $\frac{1}{10}$ of the grain or flour as payment for the grinding. If I happen to be around when my husband is doing the grinding, and I realize that the corn being ground is a traditional corn such as Bloody Butcher, I whisper to my husband, "Ask the farmer if we can take toll instead of cash." This way I get some good cornmeal!

Whatever corn was used to grind your cornmeal, you may choose whether to buy it sifted (bolted) or not. This is mostly a matter of personal preference. Sifting, which takes out some of the bran, gives a more even textured meal, but one with less fiber. You may want to choose based upon how you plan to use the cornmeal. I prefer a sifted meal for spoon bread but an unsifted meal for cornbread.

When I think of cornmeal, I immediately think of bread. However, *which* bread? Cornbread, the family favorite, or Yogurt Cornbread, my personal favorite? Then, too, there are the variations such as Spoon Bread, which is delicious with a pot of baked beans, or the whole range of muffins, from Cornmeal to Sweet Tofu Corn-Oat. In this section you will find Buttermilk Cornmeal Biscuits. And for an adventuresomely different, but very traditional, bread, try Salt-Rising Bread.

Breads are not the only things to make with cornmeal. Start the day with Crunchy Cornmeal or Tender Cornmeal Pancakes or a bowl of Cornmeal Mush. For a snack try Corn Chips, and for a showy dinner roll try Corn Bubble Ring.

CORNBREAD

Cornbread and beans are a traditional West Virginia/Appalachian meal, a combination that is sure to please. This cornbread recipe is a traditional one and a favorite in our extended family. However, it is comparatively high in fat and sugar, and thus does not qualify as an unquestionably healthy food. But try it for special occasions.

Yield: 9" x 13" pan (24 pieces)

½ cup margarine (melted)
1½ cups brown sugar
2 cups cornmeal
2½ cups flour

½ tsp. salt
2 tsp. baking soda
1½ cups buttermilk
2 eggs

1. Melt margarine.
2. Sift together brown sugar, cornmeal, flour, salt, and baking soda.
3. Beat together buttermilk and eggs.
4. Add margarine and egg mixture to dry ingredients. Mix briefly.
5. Pour into a greased 9" x 13" pan.
6. Bake at 350° for 25-35 minutes. Serve while warm.
7. Leftover cornbread is delicious split, toasted, and buttered.

"Some folks would dry sweet corn and bring it in for grinding; others would roast field corn in the oven and have it ground. Um! It smelled so good when it was ground."
—Joe Mininger, Miller

CORTLAND ACRES CORNBREAD

As a dietitian I, Mary Beth, do consulting work at a nursing home. Cornbread is one of the residents' favorite breads. So I asked the cooks for their recipe. Here it is.

Yield: 32 servings!

3½ cups cornmeal
5 cups flour
½ cup sugar
4 tsp. salt
5 Tbsp. baking powder

5 eggs
½ cup oil
1½ cups instant nonfat dry milk
1 qt. water

1. Combine dry ingredients in large bowl. Mix well.
2. Combine liquid ingredients in separate bowl and mix well.
3. Add liquid ingredients to dry ingredients and mix well.
4. Pour into greased 12" x 20" pan.
5. Bake at 400° for 45 minutes.

In early colonial days, corn was more plentiful than wheat, so cornbread was more common than wheat bread. When pioneers traveled, they carried cornbread for sustenance. That's why it was originally called "journeycake."

After roads and taverns were built and stagecoaches carried passengers, it came to be known as "johnnycake." Some called it "Shawnee cake" after the Indian tribe who probably first taught the settlers how to make it.

YOGURT CORNBREAD

There is no oil or sugar in this recipe! It is especially good baked in a cast-iron skillet. The cornbread will be crusty and chewy— my favorite!

Yield: Serves 7-9

1 cup cornmeal
⅓ cup flour
1 tsp. baking powder
1 tsp. salt

½ tsp. baking soda
1 egg
1 cup plain yogurt

1. Sift dry ingredients together.
2. Add egg and yogurt. Mix well.
3. Pour batter into a well greased 9" cast-iron skillet. (An 8" square pan will also work.)
4. Bake at 400° for 20 minutes.

Iron deficiency anemia was almost unknown in our country until we got rid of our cast-iron skillets in favor of Teflon-coated pans. Even today, I counsel my iron-deficient clients to ask their grandparents or go to auctions and flea markets for old cast-iron skillets.

Cook everything you can in these skillets. Some of the iron comes off into the food and you have an iron-fortified dish!

Still like the ease of a Teflon pan? If you properly season your cast-iron skillets, they work as well as any Teflon pan. To season: Clean pan well, rinse, and dry thoroughly. Rub generously with a non-salted fat or oil. Place in 325° oven for 15 minutes. Apply second coat of oil and return skillet to oven for another 15 minutes. A third coat can be applied if needed.

SKILLET CUSTARD CORNBREAD

A stranger on her way to Texas stayed in our home one night while we were living in Mississippi. At the supper table that evening she learned of my love for baking with whole grain flours. One day, weeks after she left, I received this recipe in the mail. Dust off that old iron skillet—you're in for a treat!

Yield: 9" round cornbread

2 Tbsp. margarine	1¼ tsp. salt
1⅓ cups cornmeal	1 cup milk
⅓ cup flour	2 eggs
1 tsp. baking powder	1 cup buttermilk
3 Tbsp. sugar	1 more cup milk

1. Heat oven to 400°. Place margarine in a 9" iron skillet and melt in oven.
2. Meanwhile, in bowl sift cornmeal, flour, baking powder, sugar, and salt.
3. Add 1 cup milk, eggs, and buttermilk to dry ingredients.
4. Pour mixture into warmed skillet; then pour 1 cup milk over the top. Do not stir. Bake for 35 minutes at 400°.
5. Allow to set for 5 minutes before cutting into wedges. A custard layer forms on top of the cornbread. This goes well with chili, a hearty stew, or a hot soup.

Note: If you don't have a 9" skillet, a 10" skillet works too—-I know because I only have a 10" skillet.

WEST VIRGINIA SPOON BREAD

A version of this recipe was first given to us by a customer at The Old Mill. Although from Hawaii, she called this bread Virginia Spoon Bread, since it originated in Virginia. But I adapted it, so now we call it West Virginia Spoon Bread.

Spoon bread, true to its name, should be served with a spoon. It is more like a soufflé than a bread. The round puff will sink somewhat after you remove it from the oven, but it will be light and delicate in texture.

Yield: Serves 6-8

1 cup sifted cornmeal
3 cups water
3 eggs
1⅓ cups instant nonfat dry milk

1 cup water
1 tsp. salt
1 Tbsp. oil

1. Combine cornmeal and 3 cups water in heavy saucepan.
2. Cook, stirring constantly, until thickened.
3. Remove from heat and cool slightly.
4. Meanwhile, mix together remaining ingredients. (The eggs can also be separated, and the egg whites beaten stiffly and folded in at the end.)
5. Add the cornmeal mixture to the egg mixture. Mix well.
6. Pour into a greased 2 qt. baking dish.
7. Bake at 375° for 45 minutes.
8. Serve hot with butter and honey if desired.

"The fee for grinding in my time was to take out one-tenth of the grain either before grinding or the same after grinding. This depended on our own needs for cattle feed or for personal use for the family. We did keep a cow and some pigs. So this return from the milling was as good or better than a monetary fee for the grinding."

—Kenneth Seitz, Miller

CORNMEAL MUFFINS

When I'm in a hurry or want individual servings, which muffins provide, I use these in place of cornbread.

Yield: 12 muffins

1½ cups cornmeal	1 large egg, beaten
½ cup flour	2 Tbsp. honey
½ tsp. salt	3 Tbsp. oil
4 tsp. baking powder	1 cup milk

1. Sift dry ingredients.
2. Add beaten egg, honey, oil, and milk to dry ingredients all at once.
3. Stir just till blended.
4. Spoon batter into greased muffin tins, filling ⅔ full.
5. Bake at 400° for 20 minutes.

Variations:
1. **Surprise Muffins:** Drop 1 tsp. jelly or jam on top of each muffin before baking.

2. **Double Corn Muffins:** Add ¾ cup corn to the above recipe.

"Ma made the cornmeal and water into two thin loaves, each shaped in a half circle. She laid the loaves with their straight sides together in the bake-oven, and she pressed her hand flat on top of each loaf. Pa always said he did not ask any other sweetener, when Ma put the prints of her hands on the loaves."
—Laura Ingalls Wilder, *Little House on the Prairie*

SWEET TOFU CORN-OAT MUFFINS

A light and moist muffin that can be made in a jiffy. You can add fresh or dried fruit to this great basic muffin which has no added fat.

Yield: 12 muffins

10.5 ozs. tofu
½ cup orange juice
1 tsp. vanilla
¼ cup honey
1 banana
1 Tbsp. baking powder

1 tsp. baking soda
1 cup cornmeal
1⅓ cups rolled oats
1 cup softened raisins*
  or dried apricots
  (or other fresh or dried fruit)

1. Blend tofu, orange juice, vanilla, honey, and banana in a blender until creamy and smooth.
2. Sift baking powder, baking soda, and cornmeal into a medium bowl. Stir in rolled oats and fruit.
3. Gently add wet mixture to the dry ingredients. Spoon into oiled muffin tins.
4. Bake at 375° for 20 minutes (or until toothpick inserted comes out clean).

*Soften by soaking in warm water for 15 minutes.

Note: To keep rolls warm on a buffet table, find and wash a big smooth rock. Place the dry rock in the oven while the rolls are baking. Place the hot rock in the serving basket. Pile the rolls around it; cover with a cloth napkin. The rock holds its heat for a long time.

BUTTERMILK CORNMEAL BISCUITS

An original biscuit recipe that combines cornmeal and buttermilk to make a golden, crunchy, light biscuit. After a day of cross-country skiing, these biscuits, along with a crockpot of chili, make a quick and hearty supper.

Yield: 5 large or 10 small biscuits

¾ **cup cornmeal**
1⅓ **cups flour**
2 tsp. baking powder
¾ **tsp. salt**

½ **tsp. baking soda**
3 Tbsp. solid shortening
1 cup buttermilk or yogurt

1. Sift dry ingredients.
2. Cut in shortening.
3. Add buttermilk all at once.
4. Stir the dough until it barely comes together. Turn out on floured board and knead with very few strokes. For the flakiest biscuits, handle the dough as little as possible.
5. Pat to ½-inch thickness. Cut with biscuit cutter, using a definite straight-down motion. Do not twist the cutter. Cut the biscuits as close together as possible to avoid unnecessary re-rolling and cutting. Each re-rolling toughens the dough slightly.
6. Bake on ungreased sheet at 450° for 10-12 minutes.

Note: An empty, washed tuna can with both ends removed, a wide-mouthed jar, or the end of a one-pound coffee can all make workable, large biscuit cutters. Dip edge of can in flour before cutting dough.

"Biscuits and sermons are improved by shortening."

CRUNCHY CORNMEAL PANCAKES

A pancake with a crunchy texture, thanks to the stone-ground cornmeal.

Yield: 12 4" pancakes

1 cup cornmeal	**1 Tbsp. sugar**
¼ cup flour	**1 cup buttermilk**
½ tsp. salt	**2 Tbsp. oil**
½ tsp. baking soda	**1 egg**

1. Combine dry ingredients; sift if you wish.
2. Combine buttermilk, oil, and egg. Mix well.
3. Add liquids to dry ingredients. Stir just until flour is moistened.
4. Fry on non-stick or lightly greased griddle.

TENDER CORNMEAL PANCAKES

A pancake with similar ingredients to the above recipe. However, the mixing method is different. The boiling water softens the cornmeal, making this pancake tender instead of crunchy.

Yield: Serves 3-4

1 cup cornmeal	**1 Tbsp. oil**
1 Tbsp. honey	**½ cup instant nonfat dry milk**
1 cup boiling water	**½ cup flour**
1 egg	**2 tsp. baking powder**
½ cup water	

1. Combine cornmeal, honey, and boiling water. Cool slightly.
2. Mix together egg, water, and oil.
3. Combine these two mixtures.
4. Add dry milk, flour, and baking powder to batter.
5. Fry on a non-stick or lightly greased griddle.

HOT CORNY HUSH PUPPIES

With a name like "hush puppies," there has to be a story. Rumor has it that fishermen cooked these at their fish fries and threw them to the dogs with the exclamation, "Hush, Puppies."

Yield: 3 dozen hush puppies

2 cups cornmeal	1 egg
1 cup flour	1½ cups buttermilk
1 Tbsp. baking powder	½-1 tsp. hot sauce (optional)
½ tsp. baking soda	1 cup whole kernel corn
1 tsp. salt	1 cup minced onion
¼ tsp. pepper	

1. Combine first six ingredients in bowl; set aside.
2. Combine egg, buttermilk, and hot sauce (optional). Pour into dry ingredients, stirring just to mix.
3. Stir in corn and onion. (Do not over-mix.)
4. Drop batter by tablespoonfuls into deep hot oil (370°). Cook only a few at a time, turning once. Fry 3 minutes or until golden brown. Drain.
5. Serve immediately.

SUPER HUSH PUPPIES

Super-good, super-easy, super-quick.

Yield: 10-12 hush puppies

¾ cup cornmeal
⅓ cup flour
¾ tsp. baking powder
½ tsp. baking soda

½ tsp. salt
dash of pepper, or to taste
½ cup buttermilk
1 egg

1. Combine cornmeal, flour, baking powder, baking soda, salt, and pepper.
2. Blend buttermilk and egg together. Add to cornmeal mixture and stir until well blended.
3. Drop tablespoonfuls of batter into deep hot oil. Fry, turning once, about 5 minutes or until cooked through and golden. Drain on paper towels. Serve immediately.

Variations:

1. Add a dash of Tabasco sauce or cayenne to give these hush puppies a little zip.

2. Add 2 Tbsp. to ¼ cup finely chopped onions to the batter.

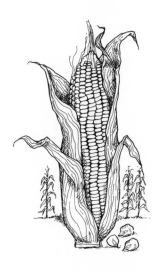

CORN CHIPS

Crackers are simple and easy to make once you catch on. We like them much better than store-bought varieties.

Yield: ⅔ lb. crackers

1 cup cornmeal
⅔ cup flour
l tsp. salt
1 tsp. baking powder
2 Tbsp. instant nonfat
 dry milk

½ cup water
¼ cup oil
½ tsp. Worcestershire sauce
⅛ tsp. Tabasco sauce
paprika

1. Combine cornmeal, flour, salt, baking powder, and dry milk.
2. Combine water, oil, Worcestershire sauce, and Tabasco sauce.
3. Stir liquid ingredients into dry ingredients. Form into ball. Knead a little until smooth.
4. Sprinkle two flat greased cookie sheets with cornmeal.
5. Divide dough in half. Roll each half directly onto cookie sheet with floured rolling pin until dime-thin.
6. Sprinkle lightly with paprika. Run rolling pin over once more.
7. Cut into squares or triangles. Prick with fork.
8. Bake at 350° for 10 minutes or until lightly browned.

CORN BUBBLE RING

A showpiece cornmeal yeast bread. Perfect for a festive Thanksgiving family dinner.

Yield: 10" tube pan of 32 rolls

2¼ cups warm water
2 pkgs. dry yeast
1½ cups cornmeal
2 tsp. salt

1½ Tbsp. honey
½ cup instant nonfat dry milk
3 Tbsp. oil
4½-5½ cups flour

1. Dissolve yeast in warm water.
2. Add cornmeal, salt, honey, dry milk, oil, and 1 cup flour. Beat vigorously for 1 minute.
3. Stir in enough flour to make a soft dough.
4. Knead for 8-10 minutes on a lightly floured surface.
5. Cover first with plastic wrap and then a towel. Let rest 20 minutes.
6. Punch down. Divide into 32 equal balls and arrange balls in a greased 10-inch tube pan, making 2 layers. Brush with oil. Cover with plastic wrap and refrigerate 2-24 hours.
7. When ready to bake, uncover and let stand for 10 minutes at room temperature.
8. Bake at 375° about 55 to 60 minutes. Remove from pan. Cool on rack. For softer crust, brush with milk or margarine while still warm.

"Love is just like fresh baked bread; it's best when made daily."
—Author unknown

RAISED CORNMEAL ROLLS

Yield: 1¹/₂ dozen rolls

¹/₂ **pkg. dry yeast**	¹/₄ **cup oil**
1 **cup warm water**	1 **egg**
¹/₃ **cup instant nonfat dry milk**	³/₄ **cup cornmeal**
¹/₄ **cup sugar**	3-3¹/₂ **cups flour**
¹/₂ **tsp. salt**	

1. Dissolve yeast in warm water. Let set for 5 minutes.
2. Add dry milk, sugar, salt, oil, egg, cornmeal, and 1¹/₂ cups flour.
3. Beat vigorously.
4. Add additional flour to make a stiff dough.
5. Turn out onto floured surface. Knead 6-8 minutes, till smooth.
6. Place in greased bowl, turning once to grease surface.
7. Cover and let rise until double, about 1 hour.
8. Punch down and shape into 36 equal balls. Place two balls in each greased muffin pan cup (or shape as desired).
9. Cover and let rise till nearly double, about 45 minutes.
10. Bake at 375° for 12-15 minutes.

Note: This recipe and the next one are similar in that they are both yeast doughs with cornmeal. However, this recipe makes a crunchier roll. The following recipe, due to the cornmeal being softened in the boiling water, is a softer and finer roll. Take your pick. We think you will like them both!

CORNMEAL YEAST ROLLS

Yield: 4 dozen rolls

1¼ cups cornmeal	⅓ cup oil
1 cup boiling water	¼ cup honey
1¼ cups warm water	1 egg
1 pkg. dry yeast	2 tsp. salt
½ cup instant nonfat dry milk	4-5 cups flour

1. Combine cornmeal and boiling water in large bowl. Let stand 10 minutes.
2. Dissolve yeast in warm water in medium bowl. Let stand 5 minutes.
3. Add dry milk, oil, honey, egg, and salt to yeast mixture. Blend well. Gradually add to cornmeal, stirring well.
4. Stir in enough flour to make a soft dough.
5. Turn dough out onto a lightly floured surface. Knead about 5 minutes until smooth and elastic.
6. Place dough in a greased bowl, turning to grease top. Cover and let rise in warm place, free from drafts, until double in bulk, about 1 hour.
7. Punch dough down. Cover and let rise a second time for about 30 minutes.
8. Shape dough into 2½-inch balls and place in greased baking pans or put in greased muffin pans. Let rise in warm place until double in bulk.
9. Bake at 400° for 15-20 minutes or until golden brown.

Note: A variety of shapes can be made from this dough. See sketches on pages 76, 77, and 87 for ideas.

SALT-RISING BREAD

Salt-rising bread, once every southern cook's pride, is now hardly known, let alone baked. But frequently we are asked, hesitantly and hopefully: "Do you make salt-rising bread?" Yes, we do. Here is the recipe adapted from our mother's own, which she got from the mayor's wife of our small Appalachian town.

Salt-rising bread is distinctive! In an article on salt-rising bread in the *Goldenseal Magazine (West Virginia Traditional Life),* Margaret Barlow says, "I have never met anyone who was impartial to salt-rising bread. Those who like it consider it food for the gods. Those who do not have many rude things to say, including likening the smell to that of the common mountain outhouse."

If the smell is distinctive, so, too, is the method. Salt-rising bread uses no yeast. The rising action is provided by the fermentation of a mixture of potatoes, cornmeal, sugar, soda, and water.

This bread, which in texture almost resembles a pound cake, is very good when toasted.

Yield: 3 loaves

2 cups thinly sliced potatoes	**½ tsp. baking soda**
2 Tbsp. yellow cornmeal	**2 cups boiling water**
2 Tbsp. sugar	

1. Mix together in a glass jar. Cover, but not tightly, and let set overnight (10-16 hrs.) in a warm (90-100°) place.
2. Next day: A foam at least an inch high should have risen on the liquid, and a distinct odor should be present.
3. Drain off 1 cup liquid. To this liquid add:

   2 cups warm water
   ⅔ cup instant nonfat dry milk
   2 cups flour

4. Mix well and let set one hour.
5. Add:

3 Tbsp. oil   **6-8 cups flour**
1½ tsp. salt

6. Mix well, adding enough flour to make a stiff dough.
7. Knead 10-15 minutes.
8. Shape into 3 loaves and place in greased 8" x 4" pans.
9. Let rise until double, approximately 1-1½ hours.
10. Bake at 400° for 10 minutes.
11. Reduce heat to 350° and continue baking for 30 minutes.

Variation: Whole wheat flour can be used for ¼ of the flour.

Mabel Titer

Grandma's Salt Risin Bread or Stink Bread
About 4 p.m., peel and slice thin 2 med potatoes
2 c. boiling water   3 T. cornmeal- white or yellow
3 T. white sugar ½ t. soda   Slice potatoes
into qt. or ½ gal jar   Add other ingred Water
first   Set in pan of almost hot water in warm
place overnite (Oven = pilot light good place)
By a.m. a foam should haven risen 1" and oder.
Dont mix until there is a foam - Drain by in
large bowl and heat & cool to warm 4 c. sweet
milk. 3 T. white sugar 2 t. soda and flour

to thicken to paste   Set in pan of warm water
& let rise 1 hr. then put flour in pan & pour
paste in sprinkle = 1 T. salt 3 c. oil or
other shortening Mix into bread dough not to
stiff just so you can knead without sticking to
your hands   Make in loaves put in greased
bread pans about half full let rise to top of
pan and bake 15 min at 375° then reduce
heat to 350° until brown about 45 min.
Grease bread on top = butter. (I sometimes use
a pkg of dry yeast to batter it raises quicker and
            doesnt taste)

CORNMEAL MUSH

Once considered "poor man's fare," this was our favorite Tuesday evening meal. Tuesday evening because Daddy didn't like it, and he was away on Tuesday evenings. We always hoped there would be leftovers so we could have fried mush the next day for breakfast.

Yield: Serves 6-8

6 cups water   **1 tsp. salt**
3 cups sifted cornmeal

1. Boil 4 cups water in a heavy saucepan.
2. Mix cornmeal, salt, and 2 cups cold water.
3. Gradually add cornmeal mixture to boiling water, stirring well.
4. Cover and simmer ½ hour. (To avoid scorching, the mush can be cooked in a double boiler.)
5. Additional water may be added to achieve desired consistency.
6. Serve hot with butter and honey or milk and sugar.

Variations:
1. Add 2 cups instant nonfat dry milk powder to the cornmeal mixture to increase its nutritional value.

2. Add ½ cup Parmesan cheese before serving.

3. ***Fried Mush:*** Mix leftover mush with some shortening: 2 cups mush to 1 Tbsp. margarine. Spread into a loaf pan. Cool. When hardened, slice mush and fry on a non-stick griddle or a lightly greased griddle. You can also place slices on a cookie sheet and broil in the oven. Broil until golden; turn and broil on other side. Serve with syrup.

WHEAT

While not native to North America, wheat has become this continent's major grain crop. The United States and Canada are two of the world's largest producers of wheat. Some of us even sing about wheat as "amber waves of grain." Wheat is the world's most important grain crop.

Yet all wheat is not the same. Between the "bleached all-purpose flour" found in our supermarkets and the warm hue of stone-ground whole wheat flour, there is a world of difference. What makes that difference? First, there are varieties of kinds of wheat and, second, there are different treatments of that wheat.

Wheat is identified as either spring or winter, based on when it is planted and harvested. Spring wheat is planted in the spring and harvested in the fall. It is usually grown in the northcentral states and Canada where the cold climate precludes the growing of winter wheat. Winter wheat is planted in the fall and harvested the next summer. Since it grows or is dormant over the winter, it needs the milder climate of the Great Plains area and the Midwest.

Both spring and winter wheats come in hard or soft varieties, depending on their protein content. Hard wheats have more protein—thus, more gluten—and work better in yeast breads. Soft wheats have less protein and more starch and perform better in pastries, cookies, and cakes. Durum wheat is a hard spring wheat used almost exclusively to make pasta. Semolina is refined durum flour.

Turning wheat into flour can be as simple as crushing the whole grains by water-powered stones—resulting in stone-ground whole wheat flour. This method grinds together the germ, bran, and endosperm. Nothing is wasted. The process is slow compared to the speed of modern hammer mills and roller mills. However, this slower speed results in subjecting the grain and flour to lower temperatures, thus lowering the risk of losing heat-sensitive nutrients. That means the flour is less likely to become rancid.

Most of the flour available in supermarkets is ground with hammer or roller mills. It is refined to remove the germ (which becomes rancid quickly, but is the source of important nutrients and natural oils) and the bran (which is coarse, but an important source of fiber). This flour is sifted several times to give a very uniform and fine texture. The flour may then be further "whitened" by aging it or by adding bleaching agents such as potassium bromate. Finally, the flour is enriched, which involves replacing some nutrients that had been removed in the refining process.

"All-purpose" flour, the most common and available flour in supermarkets today, is the attempt to create a flour that can be used for all needs. Instead of every kitchen having a pastry flour, a bread flour, and a cake flour, each in different containers, "all-purpose" flour is intended to cover all the needs, and take up only one container! It may be handy, but it signals that most of us have lost the knowledge of how flours differ and their various places in baking.

Bread flour is always a hard wheat, usually a hard spring wheat. It requires a high protein content—13-14% by weight. This essential protein is gluten. When fully developed by kneading, this gluten forms an elastic structure that captures the gas bubbles produced by the yeast, resulting in light airy bread. Other flours can be used in bread baking; however, without the protein gluten content, the bread will not rise well.

Cake flour, made of soft wheat, is a low protein flour—8-10% by weight. It is refined to be quite smooth, almost powdery.

Pastry flour is also a low protein flour made of soft wheat. It is not as refined as cake flour.

While the type of wheat has much to do with the resulting flour, it is not the only factor. I find that stone-ground flours vary from one grinding to the next, due to the wheat, the way it's ground, and the moisture. Also, the quality of the item baked depends on the weather conditions while I'm working. Warm humid weather helps bread dough rise. But pastry is easier to work on cooler days.

To preserve its quality, stone-ground wheat flour should be stored in a cool dry place. It can be refrigerated or kept in a freezer. Since the flour does not freeze into a solid clump, whole wheat flour is easy to use directly from the freezer. Just dip out the flour you need. (Warm it to room temperature when you want to use it in yeast batters.)

Since wheat is the most common grain in North American culture, we offer more wheat recipes than any other grain in *Recipes From the Old Mill*. Most of the recipes throughout this collection use some kind of wheat flour in combination with another flour. In this chapter, all the recipes use whole wheat flour; some also use all-purpose flour.

Breads made exclusively with whole wheat flour are heavy, full flavored, and hearty. This is because the bran and germ are still part of the flour. If you are not accustomed to using whole wheat flour, you may want to start slowly, choosing recipes with a relatively small proportion of whole wheat flour or recipes that include eggs and milk, which help lighten the bread. For sure-to-please options try Cool Rise Whole Wheat Bread and Rolls, Holly Day Yeast Rolls, and Whole Wheat Butterhorns. For fuller flavor and recipes that use whole wheat flour exclusively, try 100% Whole Wheat Bread, 100% Whole Wheat French Bread, and 100% Whole Wheat English Muffins. A recipe that uses 100% whole wheat flour, but is quite light due to the presence of eggs and cottage cheese, is Whole Wheat Cottage Cheese Rolls.

Also in this section are breads that call for whole wheat flour along with other grains or seeds, such as Soy-Wheat-Oat Bread, Oatmeal Bread, and Crunchy Millet Wheat Bread. Muffins especially lend themselves to a variety of ingredients. Try a smorgasbord of muffins and enjoy their variety of flavors and textures. See, for example, Whole Wheat Muffins, Wheat-Oat-Raisin Muffins, Banana Oatmeal Muffins, and Bran Muffins.

Whatever you try—from pancakes to pretzels, from rolls to popovers, and from crackers to muffins—enjoy the health and wholeness of whole grains.

WHOLE WHEAT BUTTERHORNS

This recipe has become my trademark—Sarah's Rolls! I've long ago lost count of the number of these butterhorns that I've baked, but we never tire of them.

Yield: 2 dozen rolls

2 pkgs. dry yeast	**2 tsp. salt**
1¾ cups warm water	**2½ cups whole wheat flour**
2 Tbsp. brown sugar	**2-2½ cups flour**
3 Tbsp. oil	**6 Tbsp. soft butter or margarine**
¼ cup honey	**⅓ cup chopped walnuts (optional)**

1. Dissolve yeast in water.
2. Add brown sugar, oil, honey, salt, and 1½ cups whole wheat flour. Mix well.
3. Stir in remaining whole wheat flour and enough flour to make a stiff dough.
4. Knead on a lightly floured surface for 10 minutes. Place in a greased bowl. Cover and let rise about 1½ hours.
5. Divide into 3 equal pieces. Shape into balls. Cover and let rest for 10 minutes.
6. Roll each ball into a 10" circle. Spread with ⅓ of butter or margarine. Sprinkle with nuts if desired. Cut each circle into 8 wedges. To shape rolls, begin at wide end of wedge and roll toward point. Place on greased baking sheet.

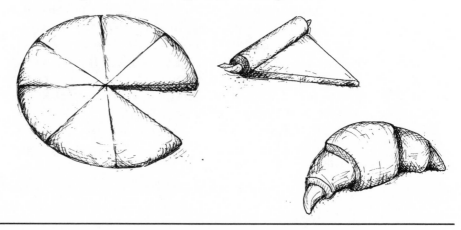

7. Cover and let rise 20-30 minutes. Bake in 375° oven for 12-15 minutes. Brush with milk or margarine while still warm.

Variation:
Before rolling up, sprinkle generously with sesame or poppy seeds.

There are no rules to bread-baking, just things to be learned.

CEDAR LAKES WHOLE WHEAT BREAD

The Mountain State Arts and Crafts Fair, one of the top 20 craft fairs in the nation, is held annually over the Fourth of July at the Cedar Lakes Conference Center in Ripley, West Virginia. For the last 20-plus years we have made and sold fresh, hot, whole wheat bread on the fairgrounds. We average over 3000 loaves in four days. All made by hand—with the help of Grandma's dough bucket. Grandma's dough bucket is a No. 8, which means it was designed to make eight loaves. We squeeze nine loaves out of it. You've been asking for our recipe so here it is.

Yield: 9 loaves

¾ **cup sugar**
¾ **cup oil**
3 **Tbsp. salt**
3 **qts. whole wheat flour**
3 **qts. flour**

7½ **cups warm water**
¼-⅓ **cup dry yeast**
(The amount of yeast varies by how hot it is and how fast the dough is rising. Sometimes the Fourth of July is pretty hot, and we have to decrease the yeast to avoid overflowing dough.)

1. Dissolve yeast in warm water in the dough bucket.
2. Add sugar, oil, and salt. Mix.
3. Add flours, and make 200 revolutions of the dough hook in the dough bucket.
4. Place dough in greased dishpan.
5. Cover and let rise 30-60 minutes.
6. Punch down and shape into 9 loaves. Place in greased 8" x 4" pans.
7. Cover and let rise 30-60 minutes.
8. Bake at 375° for 30 minutes.

While bread machines are a recent kitchen fad, bread-making aids are really quite old—witness our grandmother's "Universal Bread Maker." But we can't get away from the personal touch. Even when I use Grandmother's dough bucket, I do the finishing touches by hand. The very best "aids" will always be two hands and a heart of love.

JASON'S WHOLE WHEAT BREAD

At 10 years of age, Jason, our nephew, began to bake bread. Since he has lived all his life next door to the old mill, it is not surprising that he chose to start with Whole Wheat Bread. He first went to the mill, got fresh ground whole wheat flour, and then made the bread for his brother's birthday dinner. What a wonderful gift of love and life!

Yield: 3 loaves

3 cups warm water
2 pkgs. dry yeast
½ cup honey
2 Tbsp. oil

1 Tbsp. salt
½ cup instant nonfat dry milk
4 cups whole wheat flour
4-4½ cups flour

1. Dissolve yeast in warm water.
2. Add honey, oil, salt, dry milk, and whole wheat flour. Mix well.
3. Add enough additional flour to make a stiff dough.
4. Knead 10 minutes until smooth and elastic.
5. Place in greased bowl, turning to grease top.
6. Cover and let rise until double, approximately 1 hour.
7. Punch down. Shape into three loaves. Place in greased 8" x 4" pans.
8. Cover and let rise until double, approximately 1 hour.
9. Bake at 375° for 30-40 minutes.

Baking bread is creating a product recognized by virtually every culture as a symbol of home, nourishment, and loving care.

DATE NUT BREAD

The smell of this bread baking will draw family and neighbors to your kitchen like a magnet. Warm from the oven or toasted later, it is a memorable treat.

Yield: 2 large or 3 small loaves

2¼ cups warm water
1½ pkgs. dry yeast
2 Tbsp. honey
1 Tbsp. salt
3 Tbsp. oil
4-5 cups flour

⅔ cup instant nonfat dry milk
1½ cups whole wheat flour
1-1½ cups chopped dates
½ cup coarsely chopped pecans
1½ tsp. cinnamon

1. Measure ½ cup warm water into large bowl. Sprinkle in yeast and stir to dissolve.
2. Add remaining water, honey, salt, and oil.
3. Stir in 2 cups flour and the dry milk. Beat 1 minute.
4. Add l more cup flour and beat for another minute.
5. Stir in whole wheat flour, dates, nuts, cinnamon, and enough additional flour to make a soft dough.
6. Knead 8-10 minutes.
7. Cover with plastic wrap and then a towel. Let rest 15 minutes.
8. Punch down. Divide into two equal portions (three, if loaf pans are small).
9. Shape into loaves. Place in greased pans. Brush with oil. Cover loosely with plastic wrap. Refrigerate 2-24 hours.
10. When ready to bake, let stand at room temperature uncovered for 10 minutes.
11. Bake at 400° for 30-40 minutes. Brush with milk.

Note: Whole wheat flour may be increased to 3 cups with the flour proportionally decreased.

SOY-WHEAT-OAT BREAD

With no waiting for rising, this yeast bread can be made in a little over an hour. It is an earthy, substantial bread that goes well with soup.

Yield: 2 large or 3 small loaves

1½ cups rolled oats
4 cups warm water
2 Tbsp. honey, plus
 ¼ cup honey
 (or part molasses)
2 pkgs. dry yeast

¼ cup oil
½ tsp. salt (optional)
¼ cup wheat germ
1 cup soy grits
8 cups whole wheat flour
2-2½ cups flour

1. Warm oats in a low oven.
2. Combine warm water and 2 Tbsp. honey in a large bowl. Sprinkle in yeast and stir to dissolve. Let stand in a warm place until foamy, about 10 minutes.
3. Add remaining ¼ cup honey, oil, and salt (optional). Stir in warm oatmeal. Let stand a few minutes.
4. Add wheat germ, soy grits, and 8 cups whole wheat flour. Stir in 1 cup flour. Use as much remaining flour as needed to knead into a smooth and elastic dough.
5. Divide dough between two 9" x 5" loaf pans or three 8" x 4" pans.
6. Bake at 275° for 15 minutes. Then increase oven temperature to 350° and bake for 45-60 minutes more.

Note: If you cannot find soy grits, you can use 1 cup cooked wild or brown rice, but soy grits are preferred. Add ¼ tsp. ginger if using rice.

Long, even loaves of perfectly sliced soft white bread, so familiar in our culture, are eaten by very few people outside the United States. Two young Swedish men visited in our home while on a 6-month tour of the United States. "What are you most homesick for?" I asked. Without hesitation, they responded, "Real bread!—some that has character and substance, that you can really sink your teeth into." We made sure they tasted some "real" bread before they left our house.

HEARTY GRAIN BREAD

My friend, who recently graduated from the New England Culinary Institute, gave me a version of this recipe. While I am sometimes overwhelmed by the gourmet chef training of this friend, I find this recipe fits my style. Hearty and crunchy, this bread is delightful with soup.

Yield: 4 loaves

½ cup honey
4 cups warm water
3 pkgs. dry yeast
4-5 cups flour
½ cup oil
3 cups whole wheat flour

1 cup rolled oats
1 cup raw bulgur
1 cup wheat bran
1 cup sunflower seeds
1 Tbsp. salt

1. Combine water and honey; add yeast and dissolve.
2. Add 2 cups flour, mix well, and let stand 10-15 minutes.
3. Add oil, whole wheat flour, oats, bulgur, bran, sunflower seeds, and salt.
4. Add enough additional flour to make a stiff dough.
5. Knead until smooth and elastic, approximately 10-15 minutes.
6. Cover and let rise until double, approximately 1-1½ hours.
7. Punch down and divide into 4 balls. Cover and let rest 15 minutes.
8. Shape into loaves. Roll loaves in rolled oats and place in greased 8" x 4" pans. Cover and let rise, approximately 1 hour.
9. Bake at 375° for 30-40 minutes.

"There is no such thing as 'my' bread. All bread is ours and is given to me, to others through me, and to me through others. For not only bread, but all things necessary for sustenance in this life, is given on loan to us with others."

—Meister Eckhart

OATMEAL BREAD

Slices well for sandwiches.

Yield: 2 loaves

1 cup rolled oats	2 cups boiling water
1 cup whole wheat flour	2 Tbsp. oil
1/2 cup brown sugar	1 pkg. dry yeast
(or 1/3 cup honey or molasses)	1/2 cup warm water
2 tsp. salt	3 1/2-4 1/2 cups flour

1. Combine oats, whole wheat flour, sugar, and salt in large bowl.
2. Pour boiling water over combined dry ingredients. Stir to combine. Add oil. Cool to lukewarm.
3. Dissolve yeast in warm water. When above batter is cooled to lukewarm, add yeast.
4. Stir in enough flour to make a stiff dough. Turn onto floured surface and knead 5-10 minutes. Place in greased bowl, cover, and let rise until double.
5. Punch down and let rise again.
6. Divide dough in half. Shape each half into a loaf and place in greased 8" x 4" loaf pans.
6. Bake at 350° for 30-40 minutes. Brush with milk while warm for a soft crust.

"Bread-baking has always been a natural process—as rustic and organic as the making of wine or cheese. When bread was made at home, almost everyone knew the simple, natural time patterns that made up the method. Bread-making was just another domestic task, like sewing, milking the goats, or tending the garden. As an ongoing process, it took on a life of its own; the dough had to be watched, guarded, and responded to. This is still true . . . because bread-baking must be tempered by human care, observation, and judgment if we are to create flavorful, nourishing loaves."

—Joe Ortiz, *The Village Baker*

CRUNCHY MILLET WHEAT BREAD

Millet makes this a pretty polka-dotted loaf which is especially good toasted.

Yield: 2 loaves

2 cups warm water
1 pkg. dry yeast
½ cup millet
(you may want to
toast this lightly first)
2 tsp. salt

2 Tbsp. honey
1 cup cottage cheese
¼ cup oil
4 cups whole wheat flour
1½-2½ cups flour

1. Dissolve yeast in warm water.
2. Add millet, salt, honey, cottage cheese, oil, and whole wheat flour. Beat well.
3. Add enough remaining flour to make a soft dough. Knead on lightly floured surface until very elastic, about 10 minutes.
4. Place dough in greased bowl and cover. Let rise in warm place.
5. Divide dough in half and form into two balls. Let the balls rest, covered, about 10-15 minutes.
6. Shape the loaves carefully, dusting the board with flour to help prevent the dough from tearing. Place in greased pans.
7. Let rise again. Loaves are ready to bake when a gentle indentation made with a wet finger fills in slowly.
8. Bake at 400° for 10 minutes, then reduce heat and bake at 325° for 30-40 minutes or till done. (We've also baked it at 350° for 45 minutes with success.)

Note: Toasting the millet increases flavor and crunch. To toast the millet, place it in an iron skillet and toast over low heat for 10 minutes. Stir frequently. Millet can also be toasted in the oven at 300° for 20 minutes. Stir occasionally.

This dough may also be baked in two pie pans as round hearth-style loaves or shaped and baked as 2 dozen rolls.

HERB BREAD

Yield: 1 large round loaf

1 pkg. dry yeast
1 cup warm water
2 Tbsp. honey
2 Tbsp. olive oil
½ tsp. salt

⅓ cup instant nonfat dry milk
1½ cups whole wheat flour
1 egg
2-2¼ cups flour

**Seasonings: (select one of the following mixtures or make up
your own)**

A.
1 tsp. nutmeg
1 tsp. ground sage
2 tsp. celery seed

B.
¼ tsp. basil
¼ tsp. rosemary
¼ tsp. thyme
¼ tsp. oregano
2 tsp. celery seed

1. Dissolve yeast in warm water. Let set for 5 minutes.
2. Add honey, oil, salt, dry milk, whole wheat flour, seasoning
   choices, and egg. Beat till smooth.
3. Add enough flour to make a soft dough.
4. Knead on a lightly floured surface for 8 minutes. Place in
   greased bowl, turning once to grease surface. Cover and let rise
   till double, about 1 to 1½ hours.
5. Punch down. Shape into a round loaf. Place in greased 9" pie
   pan. Cover and let rise till almost double, about 30-45 minutes.
6. Bake at 375° for 30-40 minutes or till done. For a soft crust,
   brush with milk while still hot.
7. Cut into wedges to serve.

*Bread-baking combines physical and mental activity in a task
that connects one to living things and produces a useful product.
Providing for one's needs with one's own creativity was necessary
for our ancestors and is still true for many people around the
world today. While we do not need to bake our own bread for
physical survival, perhaps baking bread would enhance our
mental and spiritual health.*

CARDAMOM BRAID

A favorite summer picnic menu at our house is taco salad, cardamom braid, fresh fruit, and cookies.

Yield: 1 braided loaf

¾ **cup warm water**	⅓ **cup sugar**
1 pkg. dry yeast	¼ **cup oil**
¾ **tsp. ground cardamom**	½ **tsp. salt**
1 cup whole wheat flour	**1 egg**
¼ **cup instant nonfat dry milk**	1¾-2¼ **cups flour**

1. Dissolve yeast in warm water. Let set for 5 minutes.
2. Add cardamom, whole wheat flour, dry milk, sugar, oil, and salt. Beat well.
3. Add egg. Beat for 2-3 minutes.
4. Stir in enough flour to make a stiff dough.
5. Turn out on floured surface and knead till smooth.
6. Place in greased bowl. Let rise till doubled.
7. Punch down. Divide into thirds. Form into balls, cover, and let rest for 10 minutes.
8. Make three 16" ropes. Loosely braid or form into a snail shape (see page 76).
9. Cover and let rise till almost double.
10. Brush with milk and sprinkle with 1 Tbsp. sugar.
11. Bake at 350° for 20-25 minutes.

This bread is especially good warmed, but, on a hot summer day, who wants to use the oven just to warm bread? Warming it in a microwave makes the bread tough. Picnicking promotes inventiveness. We have discovered that a hot car sitting in the sun with the windows rolled up provides a wonderful place to warm a loaf of bread!

100% WHOLE WHEAT BREAD

While deliciously nutritious, 100% whole wheat bread dries out quickly. If you don't eat this in a day or two, slice and freeze the remaining bread.

Yield: 3 loaves

3 cups warm water
2 pkgs. dry yeast
⅓ cup oil
⅓ cup honey

1 cup instant nonfat dry milk
1 Tbsp. salt
8-9 cups whole wheat flour

1. Dissolve yeast in warm water. Stir and let set for 5 minutes.
2. Add oil, honey, dry milk, salt, and enough whole wheat flour to make a stiff dough.
3. Turn onto a floured surface and allow to rest under inverted bowl for 10 minutes. Knead for 10 minutes.
4. Place in greased bowl and turn dough over. Cover and let rise until double in bulk, about 1½ hours.
5. Punch down and divide dough into three balls. Cover and let rest for 10 minutes. Shape into loaves and place in greased loaf pans.
6. Cover and let rise until double in bulk, about 45-60 minutes.
7. Bake at 375° for 40 minutes. Brush hot loaves with milk.

"Let Rise until Double in Bulk"

The amount of time needed for dough to double in bulk is determined by room temperature, types of flours, amount of yeast, and extra ingredients. Altitude also plays a part. Bread rises much faster at higher altitudes.

You can test for doubling by quickly jabbing two fingers into the dough about ½ inch deep. If the dent remains and the dough feels light, the dough has doubled. If it fills in quickly, let the dough rise and re-test it in 15 minutes.

To test shaped dough for doubling, moisten finger and press into side of loaf gently with finger tip. If indentation fills in quickly, let dough rise and re-test in 15 minutes. If dough feels spongy and indentation fills in slowly, it is ready to bake. If dough sighs and seems to collapse, it has risen too long. Just punch down, reshape, and allow to rise again. Watch it closely this time.

FRENCH BREAD

These beautiful, large loaves are delicious hot from the oven with garlic herb butter or cooled and used to make garlic bread. Any leftovers make great French toast.

Yield: 2 long loaves

1/2 **cup warm water**	**2 tsp. salt**
1/2 **tsp. sugar**	**2 cups boiling water**
2 pkgs. dry yeast	**2 cups whole wheat flour**
2 Tbsp. sugar	**4-5 cups flour**
2 Tbsp. oil	

Glaze:

1 egg	**Sesame or poppy seeds**
2 Tbsp. milk	**(if desired)**

1. Combine warm water and 1/2 tsp. sugar. Sprinkle with yeast. Stir to dissolve.
2. Combine 2 Tbsp. sugar, oil, salt, and boiling water. Cool to lukewarm. Add to yeast mixture. Stir in the flours.
3. Knead 10 minutes or until smooth and elastic.
4. Place ball of dough in a greased bowl, turning once to grease top. Cover and let rise in a warm place until doubled in bulk, about 1 hour.
5. Punch down. Cover and let rest 15 minutes.
6. Punch down and turn onto lightly floured surface. Divide dough in half. Roll each half to a 12" x 15" rectangle. Roll the rectangle into a long scroll. Pinch the ends to seal. Gently roll the scroll, pulling to shape and taper into a long loaf (see page 109).
7. Place loaves on a greased cookie sheet. (If desired, sprinkle cookie sheet with cornmeal before placing loaves on it.)
8. Cover and let rise until double, about 30 minutes.
9. Make 4-5 shallow, diagonal slashes across tops. Mix egg and milk. Brush on loaves. Sprinkle with sesame or poppy seeds, if desired.
10. Bake at 400° for 20 minutes. For crustiness, place a shallow pan filled with boiling water on the oven rack below the one on which the bread is baking.

100% WHOLE WHEAT FRENCH BREAD

Yield: 2 loaves

1 pkg. dry yeast
½ cup warm water
5½ cups whole wheat flour

2½ tsp. salt
1½ cups cold water

1. Dissolve yeast in warm water.
2. Stir whole wheat flour and salt together.
3. Add yeast and cold water to flour mixture. Mix together.
4. Add at least ½ cup more cold water by wetting your hands as you knead.
5. Knead at least 20 minutes. Dough should be quite soft and silky.
6. Cover and let rise in a place that is cooler than 70° for 2½-3 hours.
7. Punch down gently with wet hands, trying not to tear the dough.
8. Cover and let rise again in a cool place for approximately 2 hours.
9. Gently punch down and shape dough into 2 balls. Cover and let rest while you prepare the baking pans.
10. Generously dust baking sheet with cornmeal.
11. Shape dough into 2 long slim loaves (see page 109). Place on baking sheets.
12. Let rise (uncovered) about 1 hour in a 70° place.
13. Cut slashes in loaf if desired.
14. Preheat oven to 450°.
15. Spray the proofed (raised) loaves with warm water. Quickly place in hot oven. Avoid heat loss from oven.
16. For crustiness, place a shallow pan filled with boiling water on the oven rack below the one on which the bread is baking.
17. After 10 minutes, reduce heat to 350°. Continue baking until done, approximately 25-30 minutes.

WHOLE WHEAT SOURDOUGH BREAD

Yield: 3 loaves

1 cup warm water	⅓ cup instant nonfat dry milk
1 pkg. dry yeast	3 Tbsp. honey
1½ cups starter	1 tsp. salt
(See recipe for	2 Tbsp. oil
Sourdough Rye Buns,	2½ cups whole wheat flour
page 94)	2½-3½ cups flour

1. Dissolve yeast in warm water.
2. Add starter, milk, honey, salt, oil, and whole wheat flour. Beat until smooth.
3. Add enough additional flour to make a stiff dough.
4. Knead 10 minutes until smooth and elastic.
5. Place in a greased bowl, turning to grease top. Cover and let rise until double, approximately 1 hour.
6. Punch down and divide into 3 equal pieces.
7. Let rest 5 minutes.
8. Form each piece into a smooth round ball.
9. Place on a greased baking sheet. Make crisscross cuts on tops of loaves (see page 110).
10. Cover and let rise until double, approximately 1 hour.
11. Bake at 400° for 25 minutes.

"A more old-fashioned and economical way of raising bread is to keep a bowl of liquid yeast on the go. It's a method that goes back into antiquity, like the custom of keeping a small firepot in the days before matches."

—Marcia Hollis, *The Godswept Heart*

WHEAT BATTER BREAD

We both have trouble with carpal tunnel syndrome, which kneading bread can irritate. It doesn't stop us very often. But, if we need to give our wrists a rest, this is a delicious yeast bread that requires no kneading.

Yield: 2 loaves

2½ cups yogurt,
  warmed to lukewarm
2 pkgs. dry yeast
⅓ cup honey
¼ cup oil

1 Tbsp. salt
2 eggs
3 cups whole wheat flour
1½ cups rolled oats
2½-3 cups flour

1. Warm yogurt to lukewarm.
2. Dissolve yeast in yogurt.
3. Add honey, oil, salt, eggs, whole wheat flour, and oats. Mix well.
4. Add enough additional flour to make a stiff dough. (Do not knead.)
5. Cover with greased waxed paper and let rise until double, approximately 1 hour.
6. Punch down and shape into 2 round loaves.
7. Place in 2 greased 2-quart casseroles. Cover and let rise until double, approximately 45 minutes.
8. Bake at 375° for 25-35 minutes or until done. This bread is especially delicious when served warm.

Batter breads require no kneading. Just stir the dough, let it rise, spoon it into pans, let it rise again, and bake. The texture is slightly coarser and the surface is not as smooth as kneaded yeast breads, but batter breads are quicker, easier, and just as tasty.

ENGLISH MUFFIN LOAF

A delightful, quick, healthy English muffin-like loaf of bread. It is wonderfully delicious toasted. Friends compare this to the specialty store-bought English toasting bread.

Yield: 2 loaves

2 pkgs.dry yeast
2 cups whole wheat flour
4 cups flour
1 Tbsp. sugar

2 tsp. salt
¼ tsp. baking soda
⅔ cup instant nonfat dry milk
2½ cups hot water

1. Combine yeast, whole wheat flour, 1 cup flour, sugar, salt, baking soda, and dry milk. Mix well.
2. Add hot water (this should be hot tap water, about 140°). Beat well. Add remaining flour.
3. Grease two 8" x 4" pans, and sprinkle with cornmeal. Spoon the batter into the prepared pans. Sprinkle tops of loaves with cornmeal.
4. Cover with greased waxed paper and let rise for 45 minutes.
5. Bake at 400° for 25 minutes.

"Let Rise in a Warm Place"

In our climate-controlled homes, we don't have the centers of warmth so familiar to our ancestors. So without the warming shelf of the wood stove, where do we raise our bread dough?

Yeast doughs love draft-free warmth—75°-85°—and humidity. The higher the humidity the more active the yeast. So:

1. Try setting the bowl of dough over a bowl of warm water.

2. Wet a kitchen towel, place it folded in the microwave, and heat for 1-2 minutes. Then place the bowl of bread dough in the microwave on the towel and close the door. Do **not** turn on the microwave. The dough will rise twice as fast, and steam from the towel will keep it from crusting.

3. The top of a refrigerator, dryer, or other appliance is often a warm spot.

4. A sunny windowsill, an enclosed porch on a hot summer day, and a closed up car parked in the sun are also warm places.

5. A gas oven with only the pilot light on is warm enough to raise bread dough.

SUN-DRIED TOMATO BREAD

The fresh tarragon gives this gourmet bread a sweet anise-like taste.

Yield: 2 medium loaves

¾ cup sun-dried tomatoes
1 cup boiling water
1 Tbsp. honey
¾ cup warm water
1 pkg. dry yeast

2 cups whole wheat flour
1-2 Tbsp. chopped fresh tarragon
2 tsp. salt
2 Tbsp. olive oil
1½-2½ cups flour

1. Pour boiling water over sun-dried tomatoes and let stand for 10 minutes. Then drain, reserving the liquid. Coarsely chop the tomatoes and reserve.
2. Combine honey and warm water in mixing bowl. Stir in yeast and let set for 5 minutes.
3. Add reserved tomato water to yeast mixture, along with whole wheat flour and tarragon. Beat vigorously.
4. Stir in salt, oil, and reserved tomatoes.
5. Add flour, ½ cup at a time, until a soft but easy-to-knead dough has formed. Turn the dough out onto a floured surface and knead for 10 minutes until smooth and elastic.
6. Place dough in lightly oiled bowl, turning to coat the entire surface of the dough with oil. Cover and let rise until double, about 1 hour.
7. Punch down and divide dough in half. Shape each half into a round or oval loaf and place on a greased baking sheet (see page 110).
8. Cover and let rise till nearly double, about 30 minutes.
9. Right before baking, dust with flour and score tops of loaves with sharp knife. Bake at 375° for 30 minutes or until well browned.

Variation:
This dough can be shaped as one loaf and placed in a 9" x 5" loaf pan. Bake for 40 minutes. It makes savory grilled cheese sandwiches.

TOMATO CHEESE WHEAT WHEELS

Something different to take the next time you are to bring a finger food to a gathering. Sure to be a winner.

Yield: 40 rolls

1 cup whole wheat flour
1 tsp. salt
2 pkgs. dry yeast
¾ cup tomato juice
½ cup water
2 Tbsp. honey

¼ cup oil
1 egg
2½-3 cups flour
2 cups grated sharp cheese (½ lb.)
2 Tbsp. chopped chives

1. Combine wheat flour, salt, and yeast.
2. Combine tomato juice, water, honey, and oil. Heat until very warm.
3. Gradually add warm liquid ingredients to combined dry ingredients. Beat 2 minutes.
4. Add egg and 1 cup flour. Beat vigorously for 2 minutes.
5. Stir in enough flour to make a soft dough.
6. Cover bowl tightly with aluminum foil. Refrigerate 2-24 hours.
7. When ready to shape, combine cheese and chives.
8. Divide dough in half. Roll each half into a 12" x 15" rectangle. Cut each rectangle into twenty 3" squares. Sprinkle about 1 rounded teaspoon cheese mixture over each square. Pat into dough. Cut squares diagonally from each corner to about ½" from center. In rotation bring the same point of each corner to center of square. Pinch points to seal. Rolls should look like pinwheels. See below.
9. Cover and let rise till double, about 15 minutes.
10. Bake at 400° for 10-12 minutes or till lightly browned.

Note: This is a great appetizer or accompaniment for a soup supper.

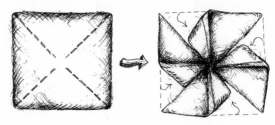

TOMATO JUICE BREAD

Slices of this bread add class to the common toasted cheese sandwich.

Yield: 2 loaves

1 cup tomato juice
2 Tbsp. minced onion
2 Tbsp. sugar
1 tsp. salt
½ tsp. cinnamon
⅛ tsp. cloves
⅛ tsp. baking soda

3 Tbsp. oil
1 cup warm water
1 tsp. sugar
1 pkg. dry yeast
2 cups whole wheat flour
3-3½ cups flour

1. Combine tomato juice, onion, 2 Tbsp. sugar, salt, cinnamon, cloves, and baking soda in saucepan. Heat to scalding point. Remove from heat. Add oil. Stir. Cool to lukewarm.
2. Measure water into mixing bowl. Add 1 tsp. sugar and stir to dissolve. Sprinkle yeast over sugar water and let stand 1 minute. Stir well.
3. Stir tomato juice mixture into yeast mixture.
4. Add whole wheat flour. Beat with wooden spoon until batter is smooth.
5. Add enough flour to make a soft dough that is easy to handle.
6. Turn out onto floured board and knead until smooth and elastic and until small bubbles appear under the surface.
7. Place in greased bowl, turning once. Cover with damp cloth and let rise in warm place till double, about 1½ hours.
8. Punch dough down and divide in half. Shape into loaves and place in greased 8" x 4" pans. Cover and let rise till double, about 45 minutes.
9. Bake at 400° for 30-35 minutes. Cool on racks.

WHOLE WHEAT COTTAGE CHEESE ROLLS

These high protein 100% whole wheat rolls are delightfully and surprisingly light. Their soft texture is sure to bring compliments.

Yield: 2 dozen rolls

3¾-4 cups whole wheat flour
2 pkgs. dry yeast
½ tsp. baking soda
1½ cups cottage cheese
½ cup water

¼ cup brown sugar
2 Tbsp. oil
2 tsp. salt
2 eggs

1. Combine 2 cups whole wheat flour, yeast, and baking soda.
2. Heat cottage cheese, water, sugar, oil, and salt till very warm.
3. Add to dry mixture along with eggs.
4. Beat vigorously for 3-4 minutes. (If using an electric mixer, beat for ½ minute on low speed and on high for 3 minutes.)
5. Stir in enough remaining flour to make a stiff dough.
6. Knead 8-10 minutes on a lightly floured board.
7. Place in greased bowl, turning once.
8. Cover and let rise till double, about 1 hour.
9. Shape into 24 pan rolls or 24 cloverleaf rolls (see page 87).
10. Place in greased muffin pans. Let rise till nearly double. Bake at 375° for 12 minutes.

Variation:
These lovely dinner rolls can have a dill flavoring. Just add 2-3 teaspoons dill weed with the whole wheat flour.

"Friendship is a basket of bread from which to eat for years to come. Good loaves, fragrant and warm, miraculously multiplied; the basket never empty and the bread never stale."
—Catherine de Vinck

COOL RISE WHOLE WHEAT BREAD AND ROLLS

This is almost no-fail! We use this bread when teaching bread-baking and in experiential meditations on bread. We have used various mixing techniques and rising schedules with success. This is truly a versatile bread or roll recipe. Have fun experimenting!

Yield: 2 loaves, or 24 rolls, or 1 loaf and 12 rolls

2 pkgs. dry yeast
1³/₄ cups warm water
¹/₃ cup sugar
1¹/₂ tsp. salt

3¹/₂-4¹/₂ cups flour
1 egg
¹/₄ cup oil
2 cups whole wheat flour

1. Dissolve yeast in warm water. Let stand 5 minutes.
2. Blend in sugar, salt, and 3 cups flour.
3. Beat in egg, oil, and 2 cups whole wheat flour.
4. Add enough additional flour to make a soft dough.
5. Turn out onto a lightly floured surface. Knead until smooth and elastic, about 8-10 minutes.
6. Choose one of the three following methods and proceed.
   Method 1: Cover with plastic wrap and a towel. Let rest 20 minutes. Punch down and shape into 2 loaves or 24 rolls. Brush with oil. Cover loosely with plastic wrap. Refrigerate 2-24 hours. Or seal in plastic bags and freeze for 1-4 weeks. When ready to bake, remove from refrigerator, uncover, and let stand at room temperature 10 minutes. If dough was frozen, thaw dough and allow it to rise.
   Method 2: Place kneaded dough in a greased bowl, turning once to grease surface. Cover tightly and refrigerate 2 to 24 hours. About 2 hours before baking, shape into desired loaves or rolls (see pages 77, 87, 108, 109, and 110). Cover and let rise till almost double, about 1¹/₂ hours.
   Method 3: Place dough in greased bowl, cover, and let rise at room temperature until double, about 1 hour. Punch down and shape dough as desired.
7. Bake at 350° for 15 minutes for rolls and 30 minutes for loaves. Place on racks to cool.

WHOLE WHEAT CROISSANTS

This is a yeast pastry which, of course, with all that margarine, dare not be called a low fat food. However, for a special occasion or with a low fat vegetable-based soup, these are wonderful! Tender, flaky, with just a touch of crunch from the whole wheat, they melt in your mouth. No need for additional spreads at the table.

Yield: 16-24 croissants

1 cup margarine/butter	**$\frac{1}{3}$ cup flour**

1. Cut margarine into flour.
2. Place margarine mixture between wax paper and roll into a 10" x 4" rectangle. Chill 1 hour.

2 cups whole wheat flour	**1$\frac{1}{2}$ cups warm water**
2 cups flour	**$\frac{1}{3}$ cup instant nonfat dry milk**
$\frac{1}{3}$ cup cornstarch	**1 Tbsp. honey**
1 pkg. dry yeast	**1 tsp. salt**

3. Mix together flours and cornstarch. Set aside.
4. Dissolve yeast in warm water. Add milk, honey, and salt. Add enough of the flour mixture to make a soft dough.
5. Knead 5-10 minutes. Cover and let rise until double, about 1 hour.
6. Punch down and roll into a 12" square. Place chilled margarine in center of square. Fold sides over margarine. Turn dough and roll into a square again.
7. Repeat the folding, turning, and rolling 3 times. Place in covered container. Chill 30 minutes to 2 hours.
8. Divide dough in half. Roll each piece into a large circle. Cut circle into 8-12 equal pie-shaped wedges. Beginning at wide end, roll toward point to form crescents (see page 28).
9. Let rise 30-60 minutes.
10. Mix 1 egg and 1 Tbsp. milk. Brush rolls with this mixture and sprinkle lightly with sugar.
11. Bake at 400° for 12-15 minutes.

HOLLY DAY YEAST ROLLS

These rolls are very adaptable. You can refrigerate them for up to 3 days. They can be made into dinner rolls, herb rolls, or cinnamon rolls.

Yield: 24 rolls

2 pkgs. dry yeast	**2 tsp. salt**
2 cups warm water	**²/₃ cup instant nonfat dry milk**
¹/₂ cup sugar	**2 cups whole wheat flour**
¹/₄ cup oil	**4-5 cups flour**
1 egg	

1. Dissolve yeast in warm water.
2. Add sugar, oil, egg, salt, dry milk, and whole wheat flour. Mix well.
3. Add enough additional flour to make a stiff dough. Dough should be soft and pliable. Do not knead this dough.
4. Place in a greased, covered bowl in refrigerator.
5. May be refrigerated for up to 3 days, if tightly covered.
6. About 3-4 hours before serving, shape the dough into desired rolls. My favorite is to divide the dough in thirds. Form into a ball. Roll the ball into a 10"-12" circle. Spread the circle with butter or margarine and sprinkle with desired herbs (oregano, basil, thyme, parsley, garlic salt, or some combination). Cut into 8 wedges and roll up, starting from the large end, to form crescents (see page 28).
7. Allow to rise, usually 2 hours.
8. Bake at 400° for 15 minutes.

Note: This dough also makes great cinnamon rolls. Just roll the dough into a rectangle, spread with butter or margarine, and sprinkle with cinnamon and sugar. Roll as a jelly roll and cut into 1" slices. Place on greased pan. Cover and let rise. Bake at 350° for 20-25 minutes.

SANDWICH BUNS

A wonderful homemade replacement for "hamburger buns," these are especially delightful with vegetarian burgers!

Yield: 20-24 sandwich buns

2 cups warm water	**⅓ cup oil**
2 pkgs. dry yeast	**⅓ cup instant nonfat dry milk**
¼ cup sugar	**1½ cups whole wheat flour**
1 Tbsp. salt	**4-5 cups flour**

1. Dissolve yeast in warm water.
2. To dissolved yeast add sugar, salt, oil, dry milk, and whole wheat flour. Beat vigorously by hand.
3. Stir in enough additional flour to make a stiff dough.
4. Turn out onto lightly floured board. Knead until smooth and elastic, about 8 to 10 minutes.
5. Place in greased bowl, turning to grease top.
6. Cover. Let rise in warm place, free from draft, until doubled in bulk, about 45 minutes.
7. Punch dough down. Let rise again until less than double, about 20 minutes.
8. Divide dough in half. Cut each half into 10-12 pieces. Form each piece into a smooth round ball. Place on greased baking sheet about 2 inches apart. Let rest for 5 minutes. Press each ball with palm of hand to flatten.
9. Cover and let rise in warm place, free from draft, until double in bulk, about 45 minutes to 1 hour.
10. Bake at 375° for 15-20 minutes or until done. Remove from baking sheets and cool on wire racks.

"Though olfactory experiences may be fleeting and evanescent, their effect on us is sustained and unforgettable. Because odors converse directly with the part of our brain that controls memories and emotional states, scent can mold our moods. It is well known, at least to real estate agents, that the smell of freshly baked bread helps sell houses."

—Ornstein & Sobel, *Healthy Pleasures*

POTATO REFRIGERATOR ROLLS

Transform leftover mashed potatoes or the "waste" liquid from cooking potatoes into moist velvety dinner rolls.

Yield: 3 dozen rolls

1½ cups warm water
1 pkg. dry yeast
½ cup sugar
1½ tsp. salt
½ cup margarine

2 eggs
1 cup lukewarm mashed potatoes
2 cups whole wheat flour
5-5½ cups flour

1. In large mixing bowl, dissolve yeast in water.
2. Stir in sugar, salt, margarine, eggs, and potatoes.
3. Add whole wheat flour and enough flour to make a stiff dough that is easy to handle. Turn onto a lightly floured board.
4. Knead until smooth and elastic, about 8 to 10 minutes.
5. Place dough in greased bowl, turning to bring greased part to top. Cover tightly and store in refrigerator for up to 5 days.
6. About 2 hours before baking, shape dough into rolls (see page 77). Cover and let rise until double, about 1½ hours.
7. Bake at 400° for 10 to 15 minutes.

Variation:
Cinnamon rolls: Roll half of dough into a 12" square. Spread dough lightly with softened margarine. Sprinkle with a mixture of 1 tsp. cinnamon and ½ cup brown sugar. Roll up as a jelly roll. Cut roll into nine slices. Place in greased 9" square pan. Cover and let rise in warm place until double, about 1½ hrs. Bake at 350° for 35 minutes or until golden. Drizzle with confectioners' sugar icing if desired.

Potato water or mashed potatoes were a favorite addition to yeast doughs in our grandmother's day. I liked the taste and texture, but wondered what it really did. Recently I read that potato water accelerates the action of the yeast.

If you store potato water for any time, be sure to scald it before using it. Potato water which has sat for a while develops an enzyme like the enzyme in unpasteurized milk. It interferes with yeast development, but it can be neutralized by scalding.

ENGLISH MUFFINS

Yield: 15-18 muffins

1½ cups warm water
1 pkg. dry yeast
2 Tbsp. sugar
1 tsp. salt
¼ cup oil

½ cup instant nonfat dry milk
1 egg
2 cups whole wheat flour
2½-3 cups flour

1. Dissolve yeast in warm water.
2. Add sugar, salt, oil, dry milk, and egg. Mix well.
3. Add whole wheat flour and enough flour to make a stiff dough.
4. Knead until well mixed, about 2-5 minutes.
5. Place in a greased bowl, turning to grease top. Cover and let rise until double, approximately 1 hour.
6. Punch down. Turn onto lightly floured surface, cover, and let rest 15 minutes.
7. Roll dough about 3/8" thick. Cut dough into 3" circles.
8. Dip both sides of circles in a pan of cornmeal; place circles on a cookie sheet. Cover and let rise about 30-45 minutes.
9. Using an ungreased electric frying pan set at 350-375°, cook muffins for 8 minutes on each side.
10. To serve, split muffins horizontally with tines of a fork.

"Knead for 5-10 Minutes"

Kneading is a process in which you push, pull, fold, and turn the dough for a designated time. Push dough away from you as you knead, rather than pushing down on the dough. A downward shove tends to make the dough stick to the kneading surface. Kneading develops the gluten, eliminates air bubbles, smooths the dough, makes it flexible, and imparts a fine texture to the finished bread.

As you knead, don't add any more flour than is necessary to prevent dough from sticking to kneading surface. A dry loaf is the result of adding too much flour. If more flour is needed to keep dough from sticking to surface, sprinkle flour on kneading surface, but *not* on top of the dough.

100% WHOLE WHEAT ENGLISH MUFFINS

Yield: 7-8 large muffins

1 pkg. dry yeast	**3 or more cups whole wheat flour**
$\frac{1}{2}$ cup warm water	**$\frac{3}{4}$ tsp. salt**
$\frac{1}{2}$ cup yogurt	**$\frac{1}{2}$ tsp. baking soda**
$\frac{1}{2}$ cup boiling water	**cornmeal for dusting**

1. Dissolve yeast in warm water.
2. In a large bowl, mix together the yogurt and boiling water. Cool to lukewarm.
3. Stir in the yeast, then 2 cups whole wheat flour, and cover the bowl with a towel. Let this sit in a warm place until doubled in bulk.
4. After the dough has doubled in bulk (about 60 minutes), mix in the remaining flour, along with the salt and baking soda. Knead vigorously, adding more flour as needed until you have pliable but slightly sticky dough.
5. Return the dough to the bowl, cover, and let rise a second time. This takes 30 minutes or more. Punch down and turn onto a floured surface. Roll it into $\frac{1}{2}$" thickness. Cut into 4" circles.
6. Dust both sides of the muffins with cornmeal and place on cookie sheets to rise until double in bulk, about 45 minutes to 1 hour.
7. Cook in a medium hot (350°) electric skillet or on a griddle for 20 minutes, turning every 5 minutes. A heavy iron griddle over a medium high burner will also work.
8. To serve, split muffins horizontally with tines of fork and toast.

Note: Almost any bread recipe with character will make holey, moist, chewy English muffins. The muffin dough should be slightly overkneaded and much wetter than bread dough. So wet your hands and knead in as much water as you can. Then proceed with muffin instruction #5-#8 above.

WHOLE WHEAT BUTTERMILK PANCAKES

The gift of a cookbook from her cousins for Christmas inspired my youngest daughter to take over the task of making Saturday breakfast. This is the recipe she uses over and over. These pancakes continue to delight us.

Yield: 9-12 pancakes

2 eggs	1 tsp. baking soda
1 cup flour	1 tsp. baking powder
1 cup whole wheat flour	$\frac{1}{2}$ tsp. salt
1$\frac{3}{4}$ cups buttermilk or yogurt	2 Tbsp. oil

1. Beat the eggs well.
2. Add other ingredients except oil and mix. Add oil and mix again.
3. Fry on hot griddle.
4. Serve as soon as possible. Do not stack pancakes.

Variations:
1. Use all whole wheat flour.

2. Add $\frac{1}{2}$-$\frac{3}{4}$ cups blueberries.

3. Add $\frac{1}{2}$ cup diced apples, $\frac{1}{4}$ cup chopped walnuts, and $\frac{1}{4}$ tsp. cinnamon.

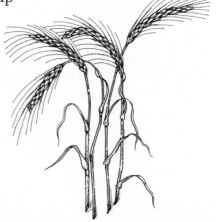

The speed of the mill-grinding depended on the method of payment. If the payment was by the hour, the mill stones turned in a slow rhythm—b y t h e h o u r. If the payment was by the job the mill stones turned briskly—by the job,job,job; by the job,job, job.

BUTTERMILK WHOLE WHEAT BISCUITS
(wholesome biscuits with NO sugar)

> This was our mother's recipe. Interestingly, as we were working on this cookbook, a friend shared with me her favorite biscuit recipe. It was one from her mother, which we discovered had been given to her by my mother. So this recipe has made a circle of friendship.

Yield: 5 large or 10 small biscuits

1 cup flour	**½ tsp. baking soda**
1 cup whole wheat flour	**3 Tbsp. shortening**
2 tsp. baking powder	**1 cup buttermilk or yogurt**
¾ tsp. salt	

1. Sift dry ingredients.
2. Cut in shortening.
3. Add buttermilk all at once.
4. Stir. Turn out on floured board and knead a half minute.
5. Roll or pat to ½" thickness. Cut with biscuit cutter.
6. Bake on ungreased sheet at 450° for 10-12 minutes.

Note: To make drop biscuits use 1⅓ cups buttermilk. The biscuits can be dropped by heaping tablespoonfuls onto a greased baking sheet or used as a topping for meat pies and thick stews. About ¼ cup sugar can be added to the batter to make a great fruit dumpling.

Biscuits are traditionally round, but other shapes are interesting and easy. Square or rectangular ones are a pleasant change. They are quicker to cut and they produce no waste. Simply pat dough into a thick square on a lightly floured surface. With a sharp knife, cut into squares or rectangles and transfer to baking sheet. Bake as directed. Wedge-shaped biscuits can be made by patting dough into a circle and cutting into pie-shaped wedges.

WHOLE WHEAT MUFFINS

A muffin recipe that lends itself to creativity.

Yield: 12 muffins

1 cup whole wheat flour
1 cup flour
1 tsp. baking soda
¼ tsp. salt
l egg

1 cup plain or flavored yogurt,
or buttermilk
3 Tbsp. oil
¼ cup brown sugar

1. Combine dry ingredients.
2. Combine wet ingredients and add to dry ingredients. Mix only until blended.
3. Fill 12 greased muffin pans ⅔ full.
4. Bake at 375° for 15 to 20 minutes.
5. Serve hot.

Variation:
Add ½ cup of the following ingredients individually or in combination:

shelled pumpkin seeds
chopped dates
raisins
grated zucchini

chopped apples
grated carrots
chopped nuts
sunflower seeds

The most important thing to remember when you make muffins and quick breads is to mix gently and quickly. Once mixed, pour the batter into the pans immediately. Have the pans greased and the oven fully heated before mixing the wet and dry ingredients. The leavening agents begin to act as soon as they are moistened.

Quick bread and muffin batters are interchangeable. Either can be spooned into muffin pans and baked as muffins, or into bread pans and baked as a bread.

Since quick breads and muffins do not require gluten, wheat flour is not necessary. Therefore, you have lots of flexibility because any specialty flour (grain or legume) can be substituted for the flour in the recipe.

WHEAT-OAT-RAISIN MUFFINS

Yield: 12 muffins

½ cup whole wheat flour
½ cup flour
1 cup rolled oats
2 tsp. baking powder
¼ tsp. salt
½ tsp. cinnamon
¼ cup sugar

¼ cup brown sugar
  (lightly packed)
¾ cup raisins
1 egg
1 cup milk
3 Tbsp. oil

1. Mix together flours, rolled oats, baking powder, salt, cinnamon, sugars, and raisins.
2. Beat together egg, milk, and oil.
3. Briefly stir together the wet and dry ingredients.
4. Spoon batter into greased muffin pans. Fill ⅔ full.
5. Bake at 400° for 15-20 minutes.

Note: While the two kinds of sugars add interest and sweetness, that much sugar is not necessary. You can omit ¼ cup of sugar without ruining the flavor.

Being frugal, living simply, and thinking economically have all been part of our heritage. Some of the things we have learned and practice include:
1. Use butter and margarine wraps to grease pans.
2. Use leftover egg wash from glazing yeast breads in pancakes, waffles, muffins, etc.
3. Use potato cooking water for the liquid in yeast bread.
4. Use leftover potatoes or winter squash in yeast breads.
5. Rinse empty honey or molasses jars with hot water, and use this sweetened liquid as part of the liquid in baking.
6. Wash and save plastic bags to use for storing homemade breads.

BANANA OATMEAL MUFFINS

This recipe comes from Esther, our brother's wife. One can count on being fed well and in style at their home. While our brother constantly teases us about health foods, thanks to Esther, he eats quite healthily himself, as this recipe attests.

Yield: 12 large muffins

1 cup whole wheat flour	½ cup raisins
¼ cup sugar	3 Tbsp. oil
3 tsp. baking powder	1 egg
¼ tsp. salt	1 cup skim milk
1 cup rolled oats	2 mashed bananas

Topping:

2 Tbsp. sugar	1 tsp. melted margarine
2 tsp. flour	¼ cup chopped pecans or
1 tsp. cinnamon	sunflower seeds

1. Combine whole wheat flour, sugar, baking powder, and salt. Add oats and raisins.
2. Combine oil, egg, milk, and bananas. Mix well.
3. Add liquids to dry ingredients and stir only until ingredients are moist.
4. Spoon batter into greased muffin tins. Fill ²/₃ full.
5. Mix topping ingredients together and sprinkle on top of each muffin.
6. Bake at 350° for about 15-20 minutes.

Grinding grains with stones is preferable to high speed steel roller grinding. The slower speed of the stones keeps the grain cooler; consequently, the flour does not lose some heat-sensitive nutrients and does not turn rancid prematurely.

At our mill, water power is used to turn the stones. So we are often alert to the weather to make sure there is enough water to power the stones. Old sayings like the following are meaningful to all operators of water-powered mills:

"Fog on the hill, water at the mill."

"Snow won't fly while the pond is still dry."

BRAN MUFFINS

These delightful and healthy muffins are a delicious way to get a lot of fiber. For breakfast, I like to crumble a bran muffin into a bowl and eat it with yogurt.

Yield: 12 large muffins

¼ cup oil
¼ cup honey
¼ cup molasses
2 eggs
1 cup buttermilk
2 cups bran
⅓ cup rolled oats
1 cup whole wheat flour

1½ tsp. baking powder
½ tsp. salt
½ tsp. baking soda
3 Tbsp. flax seeds
1 cup raisins, dates,
   figs, apples, carrots,
   or any combination of these

1. Mix oil, honey, molasses, eggs, and buttermilk. Beat well.
2. Mix bran, rolled oats, whole wheat flour, baking powder, salt, and baking soda. Fold in the seeds and fruit.
3. Combine the liquids and dry ingredients. Mix briefly only until moist.
4. Spoon batter into greased muffin tins. Fill ⅔ full.
5. Bake at 375° for 18-20 minutes.

Honey Hints

1. To remove honey easily from measuring cup, measure the oil first in the same cup. The oil coats the cup, thus allowing the honey or molasses to run out easily.
2. Honey is sweeter than sugar, so not as much is needed. Usually ½ to ⅔ cup of honey can be substituted for 1 cup of either brown or white sugar in any muffin recipe.
3. Even if honey become sugary, it is still good and can be used. In fact, we prefer this as a spread on hot bread.
4. Keep the honey container lid clean and tightly sealed because you can "attract more flies (and ants) with a spoonful of honey than a bowl of vinegar."

HOMEMADE BAKING MIX

Yield: 4 lbs.

3 cups whole wheat flour	**1½ tsp. cream of tartar**
7 cups flour	**¼ cup sugar**
6 Tbsp. baking powder	**2 cups shortening**
1½ Tbsp. salt	**2 cups instant nonfat dry milk**

1. Mix together flours, baking powder, salt, cream of tartar, and sugar.
2. With pastry cutter cut in shortening until the mixture is the consistency of cornmeal. Gently stir in the dry milk.
3. Store in tight container in cool place.
4. Use in any of the following recipes.

BISCUITS

Yield: 8 biscuits

1½ cups baking mix	**⅓ cup milk**

1. Stir together baking mix and milk.
2. Knead lightly on floured board for half a minute.
3. Roll ½" thick, cut, and place on ungreased baking sheet.
4. Bake at 425° for 10-12 minutes.

Variations:
1. Add grated cheese or chopped herbs.

2. Increase milk to ½ cup and make drop biscuits.

3. Use as a topping for meat and vegetable pies.

PANCAKES

Yield: Serves 4

1 cup milk   **1½ cups baking mix**
1 egg

1. Beat together milk and egg. Stir in baking mix.
2. Fry on non-stick or lightly greased griddle.

COFFEE CAKE

Yield: Serves 6

⅓ cup milk   **½ cup brown sugar**
1 egg   **3 Tbsp. margarine**
¼ cup sugar   **½ tsp. cinnamon**
2¼ cups baking mix **¼ cup chopped nuts (optional)**

1. Beat together milk and egg.
2. Add sugar and baking mix. Mix well.
3. Pour batter into a greased 8" square baking pan.
4. Combine the brown sugar, margarine, cinnamon, and chopped nuts. Sprinkle over the batter.
5. Bake at 375° for 25 minutes.

MUFFINS

Yield: 12 muffins

1 egg	**2 Tbsp. sugar**
1 cup milk	**3 cups baking mix**

1. Beat together egg, milk, and sugar.
2. Add baking mix and stir just until moist.
3. Spoon into greased muffin pans.
4. Bake at 425° for 20 minutes.

Variations:

Add ½ cup additional ingredients selected from one or more of the following:

chopped nuts or seeds
fresh fruit, such as chopped apples or blueberries
dried fruit, such as raisins, prunes, or apricots
grated vegetables, such as carrots or zucchini

DUMPLINGS

Yield: 5 dumplings

1 cup baking mix	**⅓ cup milk**

Combine baking mix and milk. Drop heaping tablespoonfuls into bubbling stew or broth. Simmer covered for 10 minutes and continue cooking for an additional 10 minutes uncovered.

COBBLER

Yield: 4-6 servings

4 cups berries
½ tsp. lemon juice
1 Tbsp. honey
2 Tbsp. water

1 Tbsp. flour
1 cup baking mix
⅓ cup milk

1. Place berries in greased 9" square baking dish.
2. Sprinkle lemon juice, honey, water, and flour over berries.
3. Combine baking mix and milk. Spoon on top of fruit. Bake at 350° for 40 minutes. Serve warm with cold milk.

I enjoy backpacking. One of my favorite and famous backpacking desserts is huckleberry dumplings. I make them using the fresh wild huckleberries we pick as we hike. Cook the berries in water and sugar. Add sweetened drop biscuits, and cook until done. Note: there are no measurements when you backpack!

WHOLE WHEAT ORANGE QUICK BREAD

Breads leavened with baking powder or soda instead of yeast are called "quick" breads, for good reason. They are.

Yield: 8" x 4" loaf

1½ **cups whole wheat flour**	¾ **cup orange juice**
1½ **cups flour**	½ **cup skim milk**
⅔ **cup sugar**	½ **cup cooking oil**
1-2 **Tbsp. grated orange peel**	1 **egg**
2 **tsp. baking powder**	½ **cup chopped nuts (optional)**
½ **tsp. salt**	

1. Combine flours, sugar, orange peel, baking powder, and salt in large bowl.
2. Add orange juice, milk, oil, egg, and nuts (optional). Stir until dry particles are moistened, about 70 strokes. Pour batter into greased 8" x 4" loaf pan.
3. Sprinkle with mixture of 1 Tbsp. sugar and 1 tsp. cinnamon.
4. Bake at 350° for 60-65 minutes, or until toothpick inserted in center comes out clean.

Freezing Breads

Bread products keep best at room temperature. However, bread will keep well for several weeks in the freezer. Quick breads especially freeze well. Slice bread before freezing, because this makes it possible to remove individual slices without waiting for the whole loaf to thaw. Wrap the slices in air-tight, freezer-suitable packaging. I use double plastic bags.

To thaw: Keep in packaging. Never shake the ice crystals from the package. This moisture is needed for a quality product. Thaw at room temperature. Microwave-thawing is not recommended because the bread will dry out and be overheated quickly.

WHOLE WHEAT BANANA NUT BREAD

A favorite quick bread, delicious served fresh or toasted. Slice and freeze overripe bananas in 1 cup portions for making this bread on a moment's notice.

Yield: 8" x 4" loaf

⅔ cup brown sugar	½ tsp. baking soda
½ cup oil	½ tsp. salt
2 eggs	½ cup nuts
1 cup flour	1 cup mashed bananas
1 cup whole wheat flour	2 Tbsp. yogurt
1½ tsp. baking powder	

1. Beat the brown sugar and oil together. Add eggs and continue to beat until thoroughly combined.
2. Sift together flours, baking powder, baking soda, and salt. Stir in nuts.
3. Combine bananas and yogurt, stirring just enough to mix.
4. Add dry ingredients alternately with the banana mixture to the egg mixture, stirring just enough to combine.
5. Turn into a lightly greased 8" x 4" loaf pan.
6. Bake at 350° for 45-55 minutes, or until a toothpick inserted in the center comes out clean.
7. Allow to cool in pan for 5-10 minutes; then turn out onto wire racks and complete cooling.

WHEAT HOLLOWS

My middle daughter calls these popovers "wheat hollows," because of the cavities that form in the center as they puff up in the oven.

Yield: 7 large or 12 small popovers

½ **cup whole wheat flour**	**1 cup milk**
¾ **cup flour**	**1 Tbsp. oil (optional)**
½ **tsp. salt**	**2 eggs**

1. Combine flours, salt, milk, and oil (if desired).
2. Add eggs one at a time, beating only until blended.
3. Pour batter into greased custard cups, muffin tins, or popover tins until half, or more than half, full.
4. Bake at 450° for 15 minutes, then lower heat to 350° and bake approximately 15 minutes longer. Don't peek while baking. Remove from oven and prick tops with a toothpick to allow steam to escape.
5. Serve piping hot, puffed up, and ready to eat with your favorite jam. They are also good filled with chicken salad or served with chicken a la king.

The first time I made popovers was on our honeymoon. We rented a cabin in the mountains of West Virginia and were doing most of our own cooking. I wanted to make some bread, but, since we didn't have any staples such as baking powder, baking soda, or yeast, I was trying to find a recipe for bread which took only eggs for leavening. I stumbled across a recipe for popovers.

Popovers are a quick bread, leavened only by eggs. In the heat of the oven they expand to double their size, filling with hot air. This leaves them crisp on the outside and hollow on the inside.

Heating the pan before baking the popovers gives them a crisp crust. A cool pan gives a softer crust. Whichever you choose, do NOT open the oven during baking, or the popovers will fall.

TOASTY WHEAT OAT CRACKERS

Yield: About ¹/₂ lb. crackers

1 cup oat flour (see below)
1 cup whole wheat flour
1 Tbsp. brown sugar
1 Tbsp. sesame seeds

1 tsp. salt or garlic salt
3 Tbsp. margarine
¹/₂ cup water

1. Combine flours, brown sugar, sesame seeds, and salt.
2. Cut in margarine till mixture resembles coarse crumbs.
3. Mix in water till dry ingredients are moistened.
4. Shape dough into a 9" x 1¹/₂" log. Wrap and chill several hours.
5. Slice ¹/₈" thick. Place slices on ungreased baking sheet. Flatten till very thin with tines of fork.
6. Bake at 375° for 12-15 minutes, or till edges brown. Cool on rack.

Note: To make oat flour—place 1¹/₄ cups rolled oats in a blender or food processor. Cover. Process 60 seconds or till evenly ground. Makes about 1 cup.

Tips for Making Crackers

1. It is a good idea to prick crackers with a fork before baking. This helps keep them flat on the cookie sheet.
2. Turn the baking sheets halfway through the baking time to ensure more even baking.
3. Check the crackers a few minutes before they are supposed to be done. Remove any early finishers (especially those along the edges), and bake the rest longer.
4. Crackers are done when they have a golden brown bottom and are just beginning to brown around the edges.
5. Crackers, if adequately baked, will harden as they cool.
6. A pizza cutter works well to cut the crackers. This prevents dragging the dough while cutting.

WHOLE WHEAT SODA CRACKERS

Once you've tasted homemade crackers, you may never reach for a box in the supermarket again.

Yield: ³/₄ lb. crackers

1 cup flour
1 cup whole wheat flour
1 tsp. salt

³/₄ tsp. baking soda
2 Tbsp. margarine
²/₃ cup yogurt or buttermilk

1. Combine flours, salt, and baking soda.
2. Cut in margarine.
3. Stir in ²/₃ cup yogurt or buttermilk.
4. Shape dough into a ball and knead a few strokes.
5. Divide dough in half. Round each piece into a ball.
6. Place ball of dough on greased, flat baking sheet. Cover with waxed paper and roll until very thin. Place a damp cloth under the baking sheet to stabilize it while rolling.
7. Cut into 1½" squares. Use a pizza cutter to prevent dragging the dough.
8. Sprinkle with salt and prick with fork.
9. Repeat the process for the second ball of dough.
10. Bake at 375° for 10-12 minutes, or until crackers are dry and lightly browned. Crackers harden as they cool. Cool on racks or brown paper.

Variation:
Sprinkle with a choice of garlic salt, paprika, onion salt, or crushed dill weed before baking.

CHEESE TRIANGLES

We love these crackers. They are great for parties. The triangle shape is only a suggestion. Cut your crackers anyway you please. Part of the appeal of homemade crackers is their lack of uniformity.

Yield: About ²/₃ lb. crackers

l cup grated sharp cheese
¹/₂ tsp. salt
dash pepper
1 cup flour

¹/₄ cup whole wheat flour
¹/₄ cup margarine
¹/₄ cup milk
sesame seeds

1. Combine cheese, salt, pepper, and flours.
2. Cut in margarine.
3. Sprinkle with milk.
4. Toss with fork.
5. Form into ball. Roll dough out between 2 sheets of waxed paper until about ¹/₈" thick.
6. Sprinkle generously with sesame seeds. Press seeds gently into dough by running rolling pin over dough again.
7. Cut into 2" squares and then into triangles. Prick each cracker twice. Place on ungreased cookie sheet.
8. Bake at 375° for 10 minutes or until golden.

Using Leftover Breads and Crackers to Make Crumbs

Dry bread thoroughly in a 250° oven. Stir occasionally until thoroughly dry. Cool and crush. To crush, whirl in a blender or place in a plastic bag and crush with a rolling pin. Put crumbs through a coarse sieve. Toss the hard pieces to the birds. Put the fine crumbs in a tight container and use in meat loaf, patties, or croquettes, or to top *au gratin* dishes or casseroles. Bread and cracker crumbs can be used in the Seasoned Crumb Mix for coating fish or chicken; see page 205.

WHEAT THINS

Here is a basic wheat cracker that is easy to customize with your choice of seeds or herbs added to the dough or sprinkled on top.

Yield: ¾ lb. crackers

2 cups whole wheat flour	**2 Tbsp. instant nonfat dry milk**
2 Tbsp. raw wheat germ	**6 Tbsp. margarine**
1 tsp. salt	**½ cup water**
1 tsp. baking powder	**1 Tbsp. dark molasses**
2 Tbsp. brown sugar	**herbs, salt, or seeds**

1. Combine whole wheat flour, wheat germ, salt, baking powder, brown sugar, and dry milk.
2. Cut in margarine.
3. Combine water and molasses. Add to dry ingredients.
4. Knead a little until smooth.
5. Grease two cookie sheets.
6. Divide dough in half. Roll each half out between 2 sheets of waxed paper until dime-thin.
7. Transfer dough to cookie sheets.
8. Sprinkle lightly with your choice of herbs, salt, or seeds. Run rolling pin over once more.
9. Cut into small squares. Prick with fork.
10. Bake at 350° for 10 minutes or until lightly browned.
11. Transfer crackers to a rack and cool thoroughly before storing in a sealed container.

GRAHAM CRACKERS

Yield: About 60 crackers

3½ cups whole wheat flour
¼ tsp. salt
½ tsp. cinnamon (optional)
½ cup brown sugar

⅓ cup instant nonfat dry milk
1½ tsp. baking powder
¼ cup oil
¾ cup water

1. Combine whole wheat flour, salt, cinnamon, brown sugar, dry milk, and baking powder.
2. Mix oil and water together. Add to dry ingredients and mix well. Chill dough in refrigerator for 1 hour.
3. Turn dough out on lightly floured board. Divide dough into thirds. On waxed paper, roll each third about ⅛" thick. Cut into 2" squares. Peel crackers off waxed paper and place on lightly oiled cookie sheet. Prick with a fork.
4. Bake at 375° for 15 minutes or until golden brown.

WHEAT WETZELS
Homemade Soft Pretzels
A Nonfat Snack

Pretzel comes from a Latin word meaning "a small reward." The pretzel was first made by monks in southern France as a reward for children who learned their prayers. It was shaped to represent the crossed arms of a child praying with palms on opposite shoulders, making a crisscross.

Lent, the 40 days prior to Easter, is often considered a special time for prayer and fasting. Pretzels were baked for Lent to take the place of bread. Milk, eggs, and fats were forbidden during Lent, and these little loops of bread are made only of yeast, flour, water, and salt.

Yield: 12 pretzels

How to Mix the Dough:
1. Combine:
   1 pkg. dry yeast   **³⁄₄ cup warm water**
2. Add:
   1 cup whole wheat flour   **¹⁄₂-1 cup flour**
3. Knead and let rise 15 minutes.

How to Twist:
1. Divide dough into 12 pieces. Roll each piece into a rope 12"-15" long. Work on floured surface.
2. Lay one rope in a U-shape. About 2 inches from each end, cross the dough ends. Picturing the dough as the face of a clock, bring ends down and press into bottom of the U at 5 and 7 o'clock. Repeat with all remaining ropes.
3. Dip pretzels into a solution of ¹⁄₄ cup cold water and 2 tsp. baking soda.

How to Bake:
1. Place dipped, shaped pretzels on a greased cookie sheet.
2. Sprinkle with a small amount of coarse salt.
3. Bake at 400-425° for 15 minutes.
4. Best eaten warm. Serve with mustard, if desired.

HOMEMADE GRAPE NUTS

A friend who taught me much about conserving energy serves these homemade grape nuts warm, crumbled in a cereal bowl with milk. "Why use the energy to dry, crumble, and crisp them when you're just going to soak them up with milk?" she asks.

3¹/₂ cups whole wheat flour **¹/₂ tsp. salt**
³/₄ cup brown sugar **1 tsp. baking soda**
2 cups buttermilk

1. Combine above ingredients in a large mixing bowl. Beat until smooth.
2. Spread dough ¼" thick on flat greased baking pans. Bake at 350° for 20-30 minutes.
3. Allow to cool thoroughly. Crumble and dry in a very slow oven (250°), stirring occasionally until completely dry. Grind with coarse plate on food grinder or whirl briefly in blender, 1 cup at a time.
4. Store in airtight container. Serve with milk.

WAYS TO SHAPE ROLLS AND BUNS

WAYS TO SHAPE ROLLS AND BUNS

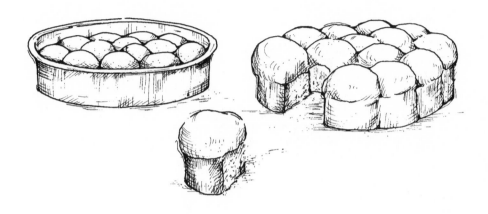

RYE

While corn has come to us primarily from this continent's Native American heritage, certain European settlers brought rye to our diet. Rye, while grown worldwide, is most common in eastern and northern European countries. Due to its winter hardiness and ability to withstand harsh growing conditions, rye was the flour of choice in these countries for years.

However, more recently, wheat flour and wheat breads have captured the major market share; good quality rye flour and breads are hard to find. In fact, recipes for rye breads are also hard to find. The recipes in this section are a collection of both old traditional recipes and new ideas for using rye flour.

Before trying the recipes, you may find it helpful to know more about working with rye flour. While it is similar to wheat flour in many aspects, rye flour has several characteristics which make it unique, especially in baking yeast breads. Rye does not have as much gluten as wheat, and the dough is stickier, heavier, and less stretchable than wheat. All of these qualities make rye more difficult to work with.

But don't let these difficulties deter you from trying. Just remember some important tips. In wheat breads, kneading helps to develop the gluten, and long kneading times are important. Kneading is important in rye breads also, but a slower, gentler, and shorter kneading is best. You may find that kneading with wet hands instead of floured or greased hands is helpful. Using water on your hands instead of flour is also useful for shaping the loaves. Probably the basic rule is gentleness, since the gluten in rye is fragile.

Rye has a knack for fermentation. Sourdoughs used with rye flour give both a tangy full flavor and aroma and also help to condition the dough. While it is admittedly time-consuming, Roberta's Sourdough Rye is my favorite recipe for rye. Without fermentation, rye tends to be alkaline, wet, and gummy. However, using sourdough is not the only way to achieve delightful rye breads. You may also use acid ingredients—sour milks, such as yogurt or buttermilk, vinegar, molasses, honey, or even citrus (see Citrus Rye Bread).

Caraway seems to be inseparably associated with rye breads. In fact, caraway is so characteristic in rye that if caraway is used in wheat bread, people inevitably assume it is rye. Conversely, if rye bread does not contain caraway, people believe it is not truly rye. If you think you don't like rye bread, try eating rye bread without caraway. You may just dislike caraway!

Traditionally in eastern Europe, rye breads were dark or "black." This was, in part, caused by the extraction of most of the "white" flour, which was sold to the upper classes. Thus, the peasants' flour was the leftovers—higher in bran and germ, and thus darker and healthier. Notice that in the Russian Black Bread, bran cereal helps to increase the dark color. Other ingredients used to darken rye breads are molasses and dark honey, carob or chocolate, and coffee or coffee substitutes.

Stone-ground rye flour contains all the ingredients of the grain— germ, bran, and endosperm. It is naturally darker than rye flour, which has been bolted to remove the bran. As with all whole grains, deterioration is a problem. Rye is especially susceptible. Fresh ground rye should be used as soon as possible or stored in the refrigerator or freezer until needed. Allow the flour to return to room temperature before using it in yeast breads.

RYE BREAD

A standard, no frills rye bread which, without the caraway seeds, can pass for a wheat bread. This is a good beginning rye bread recipe.

Yield: 3 loaves

2½ cups warm water	⅓ cup instant nonfat dry milk
2 pkgs. dry yeast	2 eggs
⅓ cup honey	2 Tbsp. caraway seeds (optional)
3 Tbsp. oil	4 cups rye flour
1 Tbsp. salt	4-4½ cups flour

1. Dissolve yeast in warm water.
2. Add honey, oil, salt, dry milk, eggs, caraway seeds, and rye flour. Mix well.
3. Add enough additional flour to make a stiff dough.
4. Knead 8-10 minutes.
5. Place in a greased bowl, turning to grease top.
6. Cover and let rise until double, approximately 1 hour.
7. Punch down and shape into 3 loaves. Place in greased 8" x 4" pans.
8. Cover and let rise until double, approximately 45 minutes.
9. Bake at 350° for 45 minutes.

Variation:

This dough can be shaped into 24-36 rolls and baked at 350° for 12-15 minutes.

An easy and especially appealing way to decorate a loaf of bread is with flour. Form the dough in the shape you want. Roll loaf in flour until coated. Set loaf in or on a baking pan, cover, and let rise. The dough's expansion as it rises creates patterns in the flour. Bake as directed. Flouring with white flour is especially dramatic on dark breads.

CITRUS RYE BREAD

The fragrance of this bread baking will draw friends and family to the kitchen.

Yield: 3 loaves

2³/₄ **cups warm water**
2 **pkgs. dry yeast**
²/₃ **cup honey**
3 **Tbsp. oil**

1 **Tbsp. salt**
¹/₂-1 **Tbsp. grated orange rind**
4 **cups rye flour**
5-6 **cups flour**

1. Dissolve yeast in warm water.
2. Add honey, oil, salt, orange rind, and rye flour. Mix well.
3. Add enough additional flour to make a stiff dough.
4. Knead on a lightly floured surface until smooth and elastic, approximately 10 minutes.
5. Place in a greased bowl, turning to grease top. Cover and let rise until double, approximately 1 hour.
6. Punch down and shape into three loaves.
7. Place in greased 8" x 4" pans. Cover and let rise until double, approximately 45 minutes.
8. Bake at 375° for 40 minutes.

Variation:
    Vary the shape of this bread by using free-standing shapes instead of loaf pans. Try hearth loaves or braids. (See pages 108-110.)

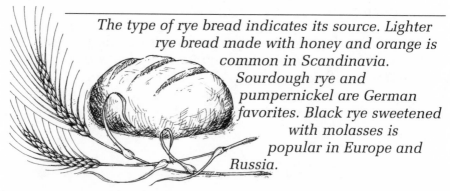

The type of rye bread indicates its source. Lighter rye bread made with honey and orange is common in Scandinavia. Sourdough rye and pumpernickel are German favorites. Black rye sweetened with molasses is popular in Europe and Russia.

CARAWAY RYE QUICK BREAD

This is a quick easy rye bread with good flavor. Its texture resembles that of corn bread.

Yield: 1 loaf

2½ cups rye flour
1½-2 cups flour
1 Tbsp. caraway seeds, crushed
1 Tbsp. baking powder

2 tsp. salt
1 tsp. baking soda
¼ cup butter or margarine
1½ cups buttermilk
1 large egg

Glaze:
1 egg white, slightly beaten   caraway seeds

1. Combine rye flour, 1½ cups flour, caraway seeds, baking powder, salt, and baking soda.
2. Cut in butter or margarine until mixture resembles cornmeal.
3. Combine buttermilk and egg. Stir into dry ingredients, mixing just until moistened.
4. Turn dough out onto floured board. Gradually knead in ½ cup flour. Knead until dough is smooth.
5. Shape dough into rope about 18" long.
6. Place rope diagonally across a greased cookie sheet that has been sprinkled with cornmeal. Make several diagonal slashes on top with sharp knife.
7. Brush with egg white and sprinkle with caraway seeds.
8. Bake at 375° for 35 minutes or until brown. Cool on wire rack.

In the middle European cultures, a loaf of freshly made bread is given to a family that moves into a new home—along with salt and candles—to symbolize good wishes for prosperity, plenty, variety, and eternal light.

Ancient people scattered bread crumbs over the heads of newlyweds, probably for the same reasons.

In ancient Egypt, bread was buried with the deceased so he/she would have something to eat on the trip to the other world.

CASSEROLE SWEDISH RYE

This light textured rye bread requires no kneading. In less than two hours it can be on the table, ready to be enjoyed.

Yield: 1 large or 2 small casserole loaves

2 pkgs. dry yeast
½ cup warm water
1½ cups hot water
2 Tbsp. oil
⅓ cup instant nonfat dry milk
¼ cup brown sugar

1½ Tbsp. dark molasses
2 tsp. salt
1½ cups rye flour
1 tsp. caraway seeds
3½-4 cups flour

1. Dissolve yeast in warm water. Let set 5 minutes.
2. In a large bowl combine hot water, oil, dry milk, brown sugar, molasses, and salt.
3. When the above liquid mixture has cooled to lukewarm, add dissolved yeast along with the rye flour and caraway seeds.
4. Stir in flour. Blend thoroughly. If necessary, use additional flour to obtain a stiff dough.
5. Cover and let rise in warm place about 40 minutes, or till double.
6. Stir dough down.
7. Cover and let rise again till double, about 20 minutes.
8. Stir down. Turn into a well-greased casserole. (I usually make two small casserole loaves, 1-1½-quart size.)
9. Bake at 375° for about 30 minutes, or until done. Remove from casserole and cool on wire rack.

"Give us this day our daily bread."

—Jesus, Matthew 6:11

FREEZER RYE LOAVES

My teenage daughter who isn't usually fond of rye bread has declared this her most favorite bread, and she has many favorites. It's a winner with me, also, because of its convenience. Frozen bread dough in the grocery store no longer tempts me.

Yield: 2 round loaves

2 pkgs. dry yeast	**2 tsp. salt**
2 cups warm water	**2 tsp. caraway seeds**
⅓ cup honey	**2 cups rye flour**
¼ cup oil	**3½-4 cups flour**

1. Dissolve yeast in warm water.
2. Add honey, oil, salt, caraway seeds, and rye flour. Beat until smooth.
3. Add enough flour to make a stiff dough. Turn out on a floured surface and knead for 8-10 minutes.
4. Divide dough in half. Form each half into a smooth round ball. Place on a greased baking sheet and flatten to a 7" diameter mound.
5. Cover with plastic wrap. Freeze until firm. Transfer to plastic bags. Freeze up to 4 weeks.
6. Remove from freezer. Place on ungreased baking sheet or in a pie pan, especially if just baking one loaf. Cover. Let stand at room temperature until thawed, about 2½ to 3 hours. Let rise in a warm place until double, about 2 more hours. Bake at 350° for about 35 minutes.

"'A loaf of bread,' the Walrus said,
'is what we chiefly need.'"

"The Walrus and the Carpenter"
—Lewis Carroll, *Through the Looking Glass*

REFRIGERATOR RYE ROLLS

Easy rolls without last-minute preparation. They are especially tasty with a ham dinner.

Yield: 2 dozen rolls

2 pkgs. dry yeast	**2 tsp. salt**
1 Tbsp. brown sugar	**3 Tbsp. dark molasses**
2 cups warm water	**2 Tbsp. oil**
½ cup instant nonfat dry milk	**3-3½ cups flour**
	2½ cups rye flour

Glaze:

1 egg white, beaten   **caraway seeds and/or coarse salt**

1. Dissolve yeast and brown sugar in warm water.
2. Add dry milk, salt, molasses, oil, and 2 cups flour. Beat until smooth.
3. Add 1 cup rye flour and beat vigorously.
4. Stir in remaining rye flour and enough additional flour to make a soft dough.
5. Turn out onto a lightly floured board and knead for 8-10 minutes.
6. Cover with plastic wrap, then a towel. Let rest 20 minutes.
7. Divide dough into 4 equal portions. Roll each portion into a 6" x 14" rectangle. Brush with melted margarine. Crease dough with blunt edge of knife at 2" intervals, beginning at 6" edge. Fold dough back and forth on creased lines, accordion-fashion. Cut folded dough into 1" pieces (see page 87). Place cut side down in greased muffin cups. Brush with oil. Cover loosely with plastic wrap. Refrigerate 2-24 hours.
8. When ready to bake, let stand uncovered 10 minutes at room temperature.
9. Brush rolls with beaten egg white and sprinkle with caraway seeds and/or coarse salt.
10. Bake at 375° for 20-25 minutes.

WAYS TO SHAPE ROLLS IN MUFFIN PAN

CARAWAY RYE PAN ROLLS

Yield: 24 pan rolls

3-3½ cups flour
1¾ cups rye flour
1 Tbsp. sugar
2 tsp. salt
1 pkg. dry yeast

1 Tbsp. caraway seeds
⅓ cup instant nonfat dry milk
1¾ cups water
2 Tbsp. honey
1 Tbsp. oil

Glaze:
1 egg white

2 Tbsp. water

1. Combine flours.
2. Mix 2 cups flour mixture, sugar, salt, dry yeast, caraway seeds, and dry milk.
3. Combine water, honey, and oil. Heat until very warm.
4. Gradually add to dry ingredients and beat 2 minutes.
5. Add 1 cup flour mixture and beat another 2 minutes.
6. Stir in additional flour to make a soft dough. Knead 8-10 minutes.
7. Cover and let rise until double, about 1 hour.
8. Punch down. Turn onto a lightly floured board. Divide in half. Cover and let rest 10 minutes.
9. Form each half into 12 equal balls. Place in two greased 9" round or square cake pans (see page 77). Cover and let rise until double.
10. Combine egg white and 2 Tbsp. water. Brush over rolls.
11. Bake at 400° for about 20-25 minutes.

Variation:
Ham and Cheese in Rye: Roll one half of the dough into a rectangle about 7" x 12". Cover dough with a single layer of thinly sliced ham, followed by a layer of sliced cheese. Roll up as a jelly roll. Seal seams and ends. Place in a greased loaf pan. Let rise until almost double. Bake at 400° for 30-35 minutes. Slice and serve while warm. Store leftovers in refrigerator or freezer.

ROYAL RYE ROLLS

The convenience of a refrigerator dough makes these rye sandwich rolls especially attractive and easy to work.

Yield: 24 oval rolls

4 cups rye flour	**½ cup sugar**
2 pkgs. dry yeast	**3 Tbsp. oil**
2 Tbsp. caraway seeds, crushed	**1 Tbsp. salt**
⅔ cup instant nonfat dry milk	**2 eggs**
2¼ cups water	**3 cups flour**

1. Combine rye flour, yeast, caraway seeds, and dry milk.
2. Heat water, sugar, oil, and salt until very warm.
3. Combine flour mixture and heated liquids. Beat for 2 minutes. Cover and let set for 10 minutes.
4. Add eggs and enough flour to make a stiff dough.
5. Turn dough onto a floured surface and knead for 8 minutes.
6. Place in greased bowl, turning once to grease surface.
7. Cover and refrigerate for 2 hours to 2 days.
8. Two hours before serving, shape into 24 oval rolls. Let rise in warm place until double, about 1-1½ hours.
9. Brush with water. Sprinkle with coarse salt and/or more caraway, if desired.
10. Bake at 375° for 20-25 minutes.

Note: To crush caraway seeds, place in a heavy plastic bag and roll with a rolling pin, or use a mortar and pestle. Crushing enhances the release of flavor.

RYE BREAD STICKS WITH CARAWAY SEEDS

These light, tasty bread sticks can be ready to eat in just 1¹/₂ hours. Children enjoy helping to shape them.

Yield: 12-18 bread sticks

1 pkg. dry yeast	**¹/₂ tsp. salt**
1¹/₄ cups warm water	**2 cups rye flour**
¹/₄ cup oil	**1 Tbsp. caraway seeds**
3 Tbsp. sugar	**1¹/₂-2 cups flour**

Glaze:

1 egg yolk, beaten	**1 Tbsp. milk**

1. In a mixing bowl, dissolve yeast in warm water. Let set for 5 minutes.
2. Add oil, sugar, salt, rye flour, and 1 Tbsp. caraway seeds.
3. Beat until smooth. Cover and let rise in warm place, about 40 minutes.
4. Stir in flour, ¹/₂ cup at a time. Then turn out on lightly floured board and knead until smooth and elastic, about 5-8 minutes.
5. Divide dough into 12 to 18 pieces, depending on desired size of bread sticks. Shape each piece into a rope about 6"-8" long. Place about 2 inches apart on greased baking sheet.
6. Cover and let rise about 30 minutes.
7. Combine egg yolk and milk and brush on bread sticks. Sprinkle with additional caraway seeds, if desired.
8. Bake in 400° oven for 12-15 minutes or until done.

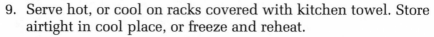

9. Serve hot, or cool on racks covered with kitchen towel. Store airtight in cool place, or freeze and reheat.

Note:
For variety, shape all or some as small oval rolls. Make a ¹/₄" deep slash lengthwise across top after shaping and before the 30-minute rising. Make your next Reuben sandwich in one of these.

DARK PUMPERNICKEL BREAD

Yield: 2 loaves

3½ cups rye flour
2 pkgs. dry yeast
1 Tbsp. brown sugar
1 Tbsp. salt
1-2 Tbsp. caraway seeds,
 crushed
2 cups water

¼ cup cider vinegar
¼ cup dark molasses
2 ozs. unsweetened chocolate *or*
 ⅓ cup carob or cocoa
2 Tbsp. oil
3 cups flour

Glaze:

⅓ cup cold water

1 tsp. cornstarch

1. Combine rye flour, yeast, brown sugar, salt, and caraway seeds in a large bowl.
2. Heat 2 cups water, vinegar, molasses, chocolate, and oil until very warm. Add to dry ingredients and beat 2 minutes.
3. Add 1 cup flour and beat 2 more minutes.
4. Mix in enough additional flour to make a stiff dough.
5. On a lightly floured surface, knead until smooth and elastic. Place in a greased bowl. Cover and let rise about 1½ hours, or until double.
6. Punch dough down. Divide in half. Shape each loaf into an oval about 8" long (see pages 109-110).
7. Place loaves on a greased cookie sheet that has been sprinkled lightly with cornmeal.
8. Cover and let rise about 45 minutes, or until double.
9. Make three or four ¼" deep diagonal gashes across tops of loaves.
10. Bake at 400° for 30 minutes.
11. Bring cornstarch and water to a boil. Brush on loaves and bake 5 minutes longer. Cool on wire racks.

DOUBLE RYE TWIST

A grand two-tone bread.

Yield: 2 loaves

2½ cups warm water	2 tsp. salt
2 pkgs. dry yeast	1 Tbsp. caraway seeds
1 tsp. sugar	2½ tsp. instant coffee granules
¼ cup oil	2 Tbsp. vinegar
¼ cup molasses	¾ cup whole bran cereal
4 cups rye flour	3 Tbsp. cocoa or carob powder
3½-4 cups flour	

Glaze:

1 tsp. cornstarch	½ cup water

1. Combine water, yeast, and sugar. Stir until yeast is dissolved. Add oil and molasses. Divide mixture into 2 mixing bowls (approximately 1½ cups per bowl). Keep warm.
2. Combine rye flour, 3 cups flour, salt, and caraway seeds. Measure out 3½ cups flour mixture and set aside for dark dough. Reserve remaining flour for light dough.
3. **For dark dough:** Dissolve coffee in the vinegar; add to one of the yeast mixtures, along with bran cereal and cocoa. Beat until thoroughly combined. Add about 2 cups of the reserved 3½ cups flour mixture and beat 1 to 2 minutes. Stir in remaining flour to make a soft dough. Turn out onto lightly floured surface and knead until smooth and elastic, about 8 to 10 minutes. Add more flour as needed. (Dough will be somewhat sticky.) Place dough, smooth side down, in a greased bowl. Turn dough to grease all sides. Cover with towel and let rise in warm place, until double in bulk, about 1 hour.

   For light dough: To second yeast mixture, add about 2 cups remaining flour. Beat thoroughly. Stir in remaining flour or enough to make a soft dough. Turn out onto lightly floured surface and knead until smooth and elastic, about 8 to 10 minutes, adding more flour as needed. Place dough in greased bowl; turn dough to grease all sides. Cover and let rise until double in bulk, about 1 hour.

4. Punch both portions down. Turn onto a floured surface and divide each portion in half. Roll each piece into an 18" rope. Place one light and one dark rope side by side (see page 108). Pinch dough together at one end. Twist together and pinch other end. Repeat with remaining dough halves. Place each twist on a greased cookie sheet that has been sprinkled with cornmeal.

5. Cover and let rise until double, about 35-45 minutes.

6. Bake at 350° for 40-45 minutes, or until loaves sound hollow when tapped with fingers.

7. Make glaze by stirring cornstarch and water together in a small saucepan until smooth. Bring to a boil over medium heat. Reduce heat and simmer 1 minute, stirring constantly.

8. When loaves are baked, remove from oven and brush immediately with hot cornstarch glaze. Return to oven and bake 2 more minutes. Remove from cookie sheets and let cool completely on wire rack.

Bread Glazes

Glazes are used especially with rye breads. Why? What do glazes do?

Glazes improve the texture and appearance of the crust. Varying the glaze can dramatically change the texture of the crust.

For example:

1. Brushing the hot loaves with milk, oil, or margarine, immediately after you remove them from the oven makes a soft crust.

2. Brushing loaves before baking with milk, evaporated milk, or egg yolk mixed with water gives a dark shiny crust.

3. Glazing near the end of baking with egg and water are common ways to give a shiny crust. For a darker crust use a whole egg or egg yolk and water. For a lighter crust use egg white and water.

4. Glazing near the end of the baking time with a cooked mixture of cornstarch and water gives a chewy, rich, glossy crust.

SOURDOUGH RYE BUNS

Rye flour takes to sourdough especially well. This starter is simple, versatile, and easy to use.

Yield: 24 buns

Starter:

2½ cups flour
1 pkg. dry yeast

2½ cups warm water
1 Tbsp. honey

1. Combine all ingredients in a crock or glass jar. Let stand uncovered in a warm place overnight.
2. Cover and let stand until sour, about 5 days. Stir twice a day.
3. On the fifth day, remove the amount of starter needed for the recipe you wish to use and proceed with that recipe.
4. To rejuvenate the remaining starter, add equal parts flour and water. For example, if you took out 1 cup starter, add 1 cup flour and 1 cup water to the starter. Mix well and store in the refrigerator until needed. If you don't use it weekly, add 1 tsp. sugar weekly.
5. When ready to use the starter, allow it to set at room temperature overnight before using.

Rye Rolls:

1 cup starter
3¾ cups warm water
4½ cups whole wheat flour
4 cups rye flour

½ cup oil
1 Tbsp. salt
¼ cup flour

Glaze:

1 beaten egg white

coarse salt
    or caraway seeds (optional)

1. Combine starter and warm water.
2. Stir in whole wheat flour. Beat well.
3. Cover and let stand several hours or refrigerate overnight.
4. Add rye flour, oil, and salt. Mix well.

5. Dough will be a bit sticky. Knead on floured surface about 5 minutes, adding more flour as necessary.
6. Place in a greased bowl, turning to grease top. Cover and let rise until double.
7. Punch down. Divide into 3 portions, cover, and let rest for 5 minutes.
8. Divide each portion into 8 balls, flatten, and place on greased baking sheets.
9. Brush with egg white and sprinkle with salt or caraway seeds if desired.
10. Let rise until double.
11. Bake at 375° for 25-30 minutes.

Tips for Working with Sourdoughs

1. Mix or store the starter in glass, stoneware, or plastic. Metal pans can cause a chemical reaction with the starter.
2. Place the starter in a bowl large enough to allow the starter to double in bulk as it ferments.
3. Never cover the container tightly, because gas needs to escape and air needs to get in to react with the yeast. Punch a small hole in a plastic wrap cover or leave the lid ajar.
4. If a clear liquid forms on top of the starter, just stir it back in.
5. Allow the starter to come to room temperature before using.
6. Use or rejuvenate the starter every 7 days. To rejuvenate without using, just remove one cup of the starter and give this to a friend or the compost pile! After removing the cup of starter, feed the remaining starter in the usual way or check the recipe. The usual way is to add 1 cup liquid and 1 cup flour to the remaining starter.
7. Starters can also be frozen. When ready to use, remove from freezer and thaw overnight.

ROBERTA'S SOURDOUGH RYE

A splendid sourdough rye, bright and tangy, with no off-flavor. This bread is amazingly light.

Yield: 2-3 round loaves

¾ cup Manuel's Rye Sour (see page 98 for recipe)
¾ cup warm water

2 cups rye flour
¼ onion separated into pieces

1. The night before baking day mix sour, flour, and water and spread the onion over the top of the mixture, pushing it down lightly into the dough. Cover tightly and leave 12-15 hours or more at room temperature.

4 tsp. dry yeast
⅔ cup warm water
starter mixture from above
3½ cups whole wheat flour

2½ tsp. salt
1 Tbsp. caraway seeds
⅓ cup warm water

2. In the morning dissolve the yeast in the ⅔ cup warm water.
3. Remove the onions from the starter mixture.
4. Stir the flour, salt, and seeds together and then mix in the yeast and starter mixtures, squeezing with your fingers until the dough comes together.
5. Knead about 15 minutes; wet your hands with the remaining ⅓ cup water from time to time until it is all used up and the dough becomes soft and begins to feel sticky. Ideally, these things should happen at about the same time, in 15-20 minutes, but they may not. Add the water very slowly. Stop kneading when the dough is soft or begins to be unpleasantly sticky.
6. Put dough in clean bowl, cover, and let rise once, at about 80°, for approximately 1½ hours. Divide into two or three small balls, cover, and let rest for 15 minutes.
7. Shape into hearth-style loaves and place on a greased baking sheet that has been dusted with cornmeal (see page 110).

8. Let rise again in a warm place until double in bulk.
9. Slash the loaves in a tic-tac-toe pattern and place them in a 450° oven. Bake with steam for 10 minutes. Reduce the heat and finish baking without steam at 325° for 40-50 minutes, or until done.

"During the time when bread was baked in communal ovens, individual families mixed, shaped, and set to rise their own breads. When the loaves were ready to bake, each French housewife would mark her own loaves to distinguish them from her neighbors'. In some regions, the family's signature or symbol—a cross, a circle, an initial—was cut on each loaf. Elsewhere a stencil was made of the family symbol, the loaf dusted with flour, and the stencil removed. In other villages, decorative patches of dough were placed on the loaves."
—Joe Ortiz, *The Village Baker*

To Bake with Steam

Place an empty pan in the bottom of the oven when you preheat it. When you put in the bread, pour one cup of boiling water into the empty pan, then shut the oven door quickly to avoid the loss of steam.

MANUEL'S RYE SOUR
(Sourdough Starter)

To Make the Sour

1½ cups rye flour	½ tsp. milk
1½ cups water	1 grain (one granule) yeast

Mix together the rye flour, water, milk, and seed grain of yeast until smooth—the mixture should be the consistency of pancake batter. Keep at warm room temperature, anywhere from 65° to 80°, in a nonmetal container that is covered to keep out intruders. Let stand for 3 to 5 days, stirring twice a day, until pungently fragrant. If the odor becomes unpleasantly sour, you have let it get too warm and should begin again.

To Store the Sour

Store undisturbed in the refrigerator in an airtight nonmetal container. It will keep much longer than anyone would think—we have used ours after as much as two months of total neglect and found it sleepy but alive. A black, watery liquid will usually collect on the top. Don't panic; it is merely oxidation, like potatoes turning dark after they are cut. Just stir the black stuff back into the brew.

If your sour has been dormant in the refrigerator and you are in doubt as to whether to use it, bring it to room temperature and double its volume with flour and water. Allow it to sit out at room temperature, stirring twice daily, until it bubbles up. Stir, and take a whiff—if the fragrance pleases you, it will certainly be good in the bread.

To Use the Sour

When you want to use the sour in dough, let it come to room temperature and give it a chance to bubble up, if it will—allow the better part of a day. Replace what you remove with fresh flour and water before refrigerating the sour again. For example, if you take out ¾ cup, mix in ¾ cup rye flour and ¾ cup water, maintaining the pancake-batter consistency.

RUSSIAN BLACK BREAD

This very dark, rich flavored bread is one of my favorites. I like to serve it with potato soup and a fresh spinach salad.

Yield: 2-3 round or oval-shaped loaves

2 pkgs. dry yeast
½ cup warm water
2 cups hot water
¼ cup vinegar
¼ cup honey *or*
  dark molasses
¼ cup oil
4 cups rye flour
3 cups flour

2 cups whole bran cereal
1 tsp. salt
2 tsp. instant coffee *or* coffee
  substitute granules
1 Tbsp. onion flakes
2 Tbsp. caraway seeds,
  crushed
½ tsp. fennel seeds, crushed
3 Tbsp. cocoa *or* carob powder

Glaze:
  ⅓ cup cold water   1 tsp. cornstarch

1. Dissolve yeast in ½ cup warm water.
2. Combine 2 cups hot water, vinegar, honey, and oil.
3. Combine flours. Mix 2½ cups flour mixture with remaining dry ingredients—cereal, salt, instant coffee, onion flakes, seeds, and cocoa or carob powder. (Set remaining flour mixture aside.)
4. Gradually add liquid ingredients, including dissolved yeast, to dry ingredients and beat for 1-2 minutes. Add 1 cup reserved flour mixture and continue to beat vigorously until well blended. Stir in additional flour mixture to make a soft dough. Cover and let rest 15 minutes.
5. Knead on a lightly floured board for 10 minutes. Place in greased bowl. Cover and let rise, about 1 hour.
6. Punch down. Divide dough in half or thirds, as desired. Shape each portion into a ball or oval. Place balls in greased 8" pie pans and ovals on greased cookie sheet sprinkled with cornmeal (see page 110). Cover and let rise 45 minutes.
7. Before baking, make 2-3 ½"-deep slashes across the top of each loaf. Bake at 375° for 40-50 minutes.
8. Bring cornstarch and water to a boil. Brush on loaves and bake 5 minutes longer. Cool on wire racks.

Shape Into Loaves

Every baker has her/his favorite way to shape loaves. We have tried several, and find this to be the easiest:

1. Weigh about 1¼ pounds of dough for each 8" x 4" loaf. Hearty breads with lots of additions may require 1½ pounds per loaf.
2. Round the dough into a ball and let rest for 5-10 minutes while you grease the pans.
3. Roll the dough into a rectangle, approximately 8" x 15". Roll up from short side. Press ends to seal.
4. Place seam side down in greased pan.
5. With a fork prick through the dough to release any trapped air bubbles.

BUCKWHEAT

Buckwheat, which probably originated in the mountains of China, is now a favorite crop in the highlands of West Virginia. It grows well in the cool moist climate of the mountains and does not require a long growing season. Another attractive feature of buckwheat is that it is a natural herbicide and so does not require much cultivation. Unfortunately for the farmer, deer find buckwheat to be a delectable feast. They can easily destroy a whole field overnight.

The name, buckwheat, can be confusing. It is *not* a type of wheat as its name suggests, nor is it even a grain. Buckwheat is the fruit of an herbaceous plant, not the fruit of a grass. The plant, usually 1-2 feet high, has branches with heart-shaped leaves and lovely white flowers. It is more closely related to rhubarb than to wheat.

Buckwheat's white flowers attract bees, which use the nectar to make a rich, dark, full-flavored honey. The pollinated flowers then form a triangular-shaped seed. This seed has a hard, black, outer shell which is stripped off either before grinding into flour or sifted out after grinding. If the flour has dark specks in it, not all the hulls were sifted out. Thus, the darker the flour, the more hull, the more flavor, and the more fiber it contains. This explains why most people prefer stone-ground buckwheat.

While buckwheat flour is high in protein, the protein is not gluten; therefore, the flour is most often used in pancakes or quick breads rather than yeast breads. In yeast breads it is heavy. A little bit gives lots of flavor, as well as a characteristic blue-gray color. Its distinct full flavor, which can be described as nut-like, works best in buckwheat pancakes, griddle cakes, and crepes.

I think of buckwheat as a winter food. With its heavy flavor and high nutrient value, buckwheat flour was traditionally used to make pancakes. These pancakes were the breakfast food from harvest in October through the winter, often made with a sourdough starter (see Buckwheat Cakes with Yeast, and Buckwheat Sourdough Pancakes).

100% BUCKWHEAT PANCAKES

These are hearty pancakes, especially good with sausage gravy or creamed chicken. They can be thinned with milk and made more like a crepe.

Yield: Serves 4

2 cups buckwheat flour	**1 egg**
2 tsp. baking powder	**2 cups milk**
2 tsp. sugar	**2 Tbsp. oil**
½ tsp. salt	

1. Combine dry ingredients.
2. In a separate bowl beat together egg, milk, and oil.
3. Add liquids to dry ingredients. Stir just until flour is moistened.
4. Fry on a hot non-stick, or lightly greased, griddle.

Tips for Perfect Pancakes

1. Stir just until flour is moistened. Over-stirring batter makes a less tender pancake. The lumps will come out in the baking. The stiffer the batter, the less mixing is needed.
2. Have griddle hot before baking. The griddle is the right temperature when drops of water dance on the surface.
3. Turn pancakes only once. Never flatten a baking pancake. You can tell when the first side is done by the broken bubbles on the top and the dry edge. Baking time averages half as long for the second side as for the first.

BUTTERMILK BUCKWHEAT CAKES

Yield: 16 pancakes

2 cups buckwheat flour	**1 tsp. salt**
¾ cup flour	**2 cups buttermilk**
2 tsp. baking powder	**1¼ cups milk**
1 tsp. baking soda	**1 Tbsp. oil**

1. Combine dry ingredients.
2. In a separate bowl mix buttermilk, milk, and oil. Mix well.
3. Add liquids to dry ingredients. Stir just until flour is moistened.
4. Fry on a hot non-stick, or lightly greased, griddle.

BUCKWHEAT GRIDDLE CAKES

This recipe came to us from the Buckwheat Festival. At this annual fall festival celebrating the harvest, buckwheat cakes are the featured food. This recipe has more than the normal or necessary sugar and fat; however, for a celebration, these are good cakes!

Yield: 12 pancakes

1 cup buckwheat flour	**3 Tbsp. sugar**
½ cup flour	**1 egg**
3 tsp. baking powder	**3 Tbsp. oil**
½ tsp. salt	**1¼ cups milk**

1. Combine dry ingredients.
2. Beat together egg, oil, and milk.
3. Combine wet and dry ingredients. Stir just until flour is moistened.
4. Fry on a hot non-stick, or lightly greased, griddle.

BUCKWHEAT CAKES WITH YEAST

Traditionally, in the fall after the buckwheat harvest, the cook made a starter and thereafter served buckwheat pancakes each morning, along with maple syrup and ham, sausage, or bacon. This recipe is a traditional one using yeast to make the starter. It is not difficult; you just have to plan ahead so that you start the night before the day you want the pancakes.

Yield: 12 large cakes

1 pkg. dry yeast　　　　　　**½ tsp. salt**
1¾ cups warm water　　　　**1¾ cups buckwheat flour**
½ cup instant nonfat dry milk

1. Dissolve yeast in 1¾ cups warm water.
2. Add dry milk, salt, and buckwheat flour. Mix well.
3. Cover and let set overnight in a warm place.

1 tsp. baking soda　　　　　**1 Tbsp. honey**
½ cup warm water　　　　　　**1 egg**

4. In the morning, dissolve baking soda in ½ cup warm water and add to sponge.
5. Add honey and beaten egg.
6. Fry on a hot non-stick, or lightly greased, griddle.

In the spring, as the days warm up and the snow melts, we drill holes in the maple trees around our house. We fashion spouts from sumac wood and drive the spouts into the holes drilled in the trees. Soon the sap is dripping out of the spouts. Quickly we position buckets to catch the sap. If it runs well, we collect several hundred gallons of sap. That seems like a lot until you realize that it takes 40 gallons of sap to make 1 gallon of syrup. So early in the morning we start a big fire under the evaporator pan and cook the watery sap all day until it becomes a sweet syrup. At our house, eating pancakes with maple syrup is almost a sacrament of spring—recognizing the gift of the earth and trees in the sap, and our faithful work in collecting and cooking it down.

BUCKWHEAT SOURDOUGH PANCAKES

This is another "starter" recipe. However, with this recipe, once the starter is made, you can keep it in the refrigerator and use it whenever you wish.

Yield: Serves 4

Starter:

2 cups warm water　　　**1½ cups flour**
1 cup buckwheat flour

1. Mix thoroughly. Cover and set in warm place overnight. (Allow 10-12 hours for fermentation.)
2. In the morning, remove 1 cup starter for next time. Store in refrigerator.
3. Before using this starter again, add the above ingredients and follow steps 1 and 2.
4. To keep starter fresh, use at least once a week.

Pancakes:

To the remaining starter add:

1 egg　　　　　　　　**1 tsp. salt**
2 Tbsp. oil　　　　　　**1 tsp. soda**
¼ cup instant　　　　　**2 Tbsp. sugar**
nonfat dry milk

4. Mix all ingredients with starter and beat until smooth.
5. Fry on a hot non-stick, or lightly greased, griddle.

Harmony between a daughter-in-law and mother-in-law may be gauged by the number of recipes each uses from the other's files!

BUCKWHEAT CREPES

Buckwheat crepes with their slightly nutty flavor make delicious dessert crepes. Try these with a variety of fruit, nut, or cheese fillings.

They can be made ahead through step 6 and refrigerated until ready to bake.

Yield: 6 crepes

½ cup buckwheat
½ cup flour
1½ cups milk

1 egg
2 Tbsp. sugar
¼ tsp. salt

1. Combine all ingredients and mix well or blend in blender.
2. Let the batter stand for 30 minutes.
3. Pour ¼ cup batter on a moderately hot (pan is ready when a drop of water dances on it), lightly greased griddle. Tilt pan to spread the batter thinly over the griddle.
4. Cook briefly—1 to 2 minutes—until golden brown underneath and dry on top. Turn and cook on other side, about 1 minute.
5. Remove from pan and cover with a damp cloth. Crepes can be stacked on top of each other.
6. Fill crepes with desired filling. Roll up and arrange crepes seam side down in a shallow baking dish.
7. Bake at 350° for 10 minutes.
8. Serve hot sprinkled with confectioners' sugar, if desired.

Variation:
Spices such as cloves, cinnamon, or cardamom can be added to the batter.

Filling suggestions:
1. *Cheese:* Mix together 2 cups cottage cheese, grated rind of one lemon, and 1 Tbsp. sugar.
2. *Nut:* Mix together 2 cups finely chopped walnuts and ½ cup sugar.
3. Peanut butter and jelly.
4. Fruit preserves or pie filling.

WAYS TO SHAPE LOAVES

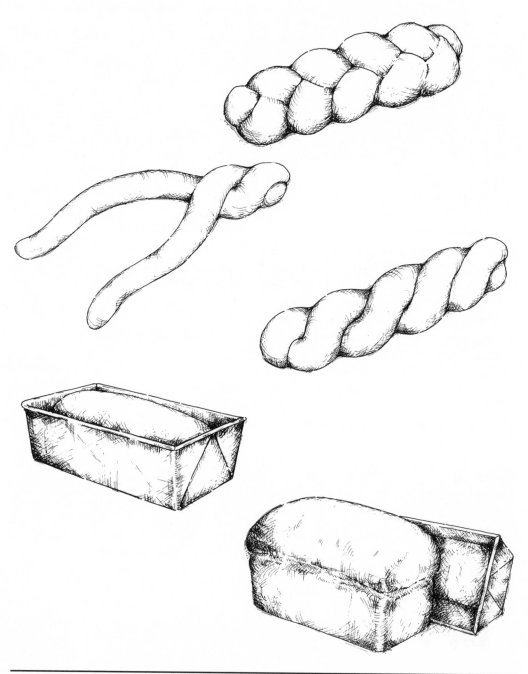

WAYS TO SHAPE LOAVES

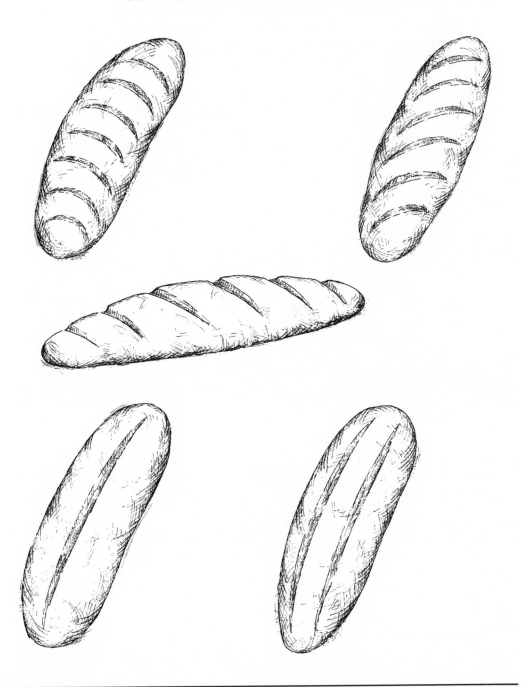

WAYS TO SHAPE LOAVES

MULTI-GRAIN

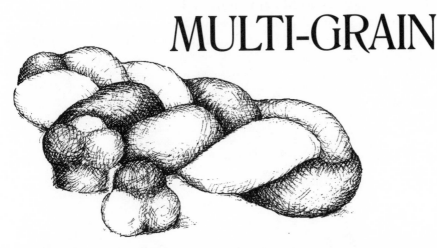

As the name implies, multi-grain breads contain more than one whole grain flour. Most bread bakers are tempted at some point to combine different grains to produce the best tasting and most nutritious bread. When, during grinding, the miller switches from one grain to another, the flour that comes out of the spout during the switch is mixed. You can discard this or use it for animal feed, but we collect it and use it for multi-grain breads. Since the proportion of the different flours is impossible to measure in this mixed grain, the results also vary.

The recipes in this chapter suggest specific proportions of each flour that blend well to produce well-balanced breads, rich in flavor and pleasing in texture. However, don't let our specifics deter you from experimenting. Some recipes, such as Basic Pancake Mix, are written especially to invite your inventiveness.

When combining flours, remember that wheat is nutty and rather sweet, rye has a grainy flavor, and cornmeal adds an interesting crunch to the crumb. Buckwheat has a distinctive tart taste and strong flavor; therefore, it is best used in moderation.

In a number of the recipes, we suggest combining whole wheat (rather than all-purpose flour) with corn to increase the nutrition and flavor of your finished product. Especially delightful in this regard are Yeast Grain Pancakes, Pumpkin Cornbread, Cranberry Cornbread Loaves, and Anadama Bread.

The combination of wheat, rye, and corn adds color to Three

Flour Braided Bread. It also adds flavor and keeping quality to The Old Mill Sampler and Multi-Grain English Muffins.

Frequently we add other grains, which are not stone-ground at our mill, to other flours. The Wheat Rye Oat Bread is one of my favorites.

BASIC PANCAKE MIX

Commercial pancake mixes are handy and easy, but uninteresting. This recipe, while also convenient, lends itself to creativity. You can use any of the four stone-ground flours in any combination. You can also decrease the all-purpose flour to 3 cups and increase the stone-ground flours to 3 cups.

Pancake Mix:

4 cups flour	1 Tbsp. salt
2 cups any stone-ground flour: buckwheat, whole wheat, rye, or cornmeal	6 Tbsp. sugar
	6 Tbsp. baking powder
	2 cups instant nonfat dry milk

1. Mix well and store in airtight container in a cool place.

Pancake Batter:
Yield: Serves 4

1 egg	2 Tbsp. oil
1 cup water	1½ cups mix

2. Beat together egg, water, and oil.
3. Add pancake mix. Stir just until mix is moistened.
4. Fry on a hot non-stick griddle.

At home, we cooked "from scratch." We used the raw ingredients we produced ourselves or the small amount of staples we purchased from the grocery store. It wasn't until we left home and started grocery shopping for ourselves that we discovered all the prepared baking mix options. That was 20 years ago. Today the choices are multiplied many times over.

Prepared foods are designed to be easy and time-saving. But what have we really saved? Is what we are eating good, let alone good for us, and good for the earth? Our bias is that, the closer we are to the production of the food we eat, the healthier it is for us. Notice where most of your food dollars go. Is it for preparation, packaging and shipping, or for the actual food?

YEAST GRAIN PANCAKES

These hearty pancakes are a delightful combination of cornmeal and whole wheat flour.

Yield: Serves 4

1 tsp. yeast (¹/₃ of a package)
1¼ cups warm water
¼ cup honey
1 egg

¹/₃ cup instant nonfat dry milk
1 cup cornmeal
1 cup whole wheat flour

1. Dissolve yeast in warm water. Let set 5 minutes.
2. Add honey, egg, and dry milk. Beat well.
3. Gradually add cornmeal and whole wheat flour. Beat well to remove all lumps.
4. Cover tightly and refrigerate overnight.
5. When ready to use, fry on a non-stick, or lightly greased, griddle.

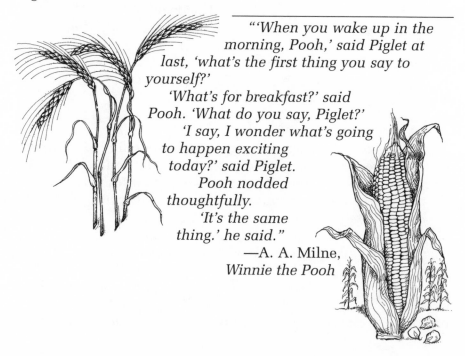

"'When you wake up in the morning, Pooh,' said Piglet at last, 'what's the first thing you say to yourself?'

'What's for breakfast?' said Pooh. 'What do you say, Piglet?'

'I say, I wonder what's going to happen exciting today?' said Piglet.

Pooh nodded thoughtfully.

'It's the same thing.' he said."

—A. A. Milne,
Winnie the Pooh

PUMPKIN CORNBREAD

Truly an autumn combination with a Vitamin A boost.

Yield: 8-9 servings

1 cup cornmeal
½ cup flour
½ cup whole wheat flour
1 Tbsp. baking powder
1 tsp. salt
½ tsp. cinnamon
¼ tsp. nutmeg

2 eggs
1 cup pumpkin
  or winter squash puree
⅔ cup brown sugar
¼ cup oil
1 Tbsp. molasses
½ cup chopped pecans (optional)

1. Sift cornmeal, flours, baking powder, salt, and spices in a large mixing bowl. (Add coarse cornmeal particles that do not go through sifter to the sifted ingredients.)
2. Beat eggs lightly in a separate bowl. Whisk in pumpkin, brown sugar, oil, and molasses.
3. Make a well in the dry mixture. Add liquids and blend batter with a few quick strokes, just until no traces of flour remain. Add pecans during last few strokes, if desired.
4. Pour batter into a greased 10" glass pie pan or a 9" square baking pan.
5. Bake at 400° for approximately 30 minutes, until cornbread is browned and the surface has a slightly springy feel.

"A very strait-laced backwoods girl does not permit a partner to put his arm around her waist at all, but is swung by a handclasp only. The two methods of swinging are known as Biscuits and Cornbread, as in this old dance call:
Meet your pardner
Pat her on the head
If she don't like biscuits
Feed her cornbread."

—Vance Randolph,
Down in the Holler: A Gallery of Ozark Folk Speech

CRANBERRY CORNBREAD LOAVES

These small, quick, delicious mini-loaves combine cornmeal and cranberries, two foods the first American settlers learned about from the Native Americans. The breads are particularly nutritious and remarkably rich tasting. A special addition to a brunch or Thanksgiving-time gathering.

Yield: 4 mini-loaves

1 cup flour
½ cup whole wheat flour
⅓ cup brown sugar
1½ tsp. salt
1¼ tsp. baking soda
2 cups cornmeal
1 cup wheat germ

½ cup chopped nuts
2 cups buttermilk
⅓ cup oil
½ cup mashed banana
2 eggs, lightly beaten
1 cup coarsely chopped fresh or
    frozen cranberries

1. Stir together flours, brown sugar, salt, and baking soda until blended. Mix in cornmeal, wheat germ, and nuts.
2. In a separate bowl, mix buttermilk, oil, banana, and eggs. Stir liquid mixture into dry ingredients just until blended. Fold in the cranberries.
3. Pour batter into 4 greased 5½" x 3" loaf pans.
4. Bake at 375° for 30-35 minutes, or until toothpick inserted in the center comes out clean.
5. Cool in pans for 5 minutes, then remove and cool completely on wire rack.

In the area of West Virginia where we live, there are several wild cranberry bogs. In the fall, we love to hike up the mountains to these deep bogs on the top. There, on a crisp, clear day, with azure blue skies overhead and a thick spongy carpet of moss underfoot, we pick tiny red cranberries. Since these wild cranberries are so tiny, they are full of flavor and do not need to be chopped before using. We think these cranberries are exceptional and so use them only in particular recipes for special occasions.

BOSTON BROWN BREAD

We heat our house with a woodstove, and in the winter I enjoy cooking on it. On a cold winter night, there's nothing better than a loaf of Boston Brown Bread and a pot of beans which have simmered all day. Add a salad or vegetable, and you have a hearty and healthy meal.

Yield: 1 large loaf

1 cup whole wheat flour	**1 tsp. salt**
½ cup rye flour	**2 cups yogurt**
1 cup flour	**½ cup honey or molasses**
½ cup cornmeal	**1 cup raisins**
2 tsp. baking soda	**¼ cup toasted sunflower seeds**

1. Mix flours, cornmeal, baking soda, and salt.
2. Mix yogurt, honey, raisins, and sunflower seeds.
3. Combine wet and dry ingredients. Mix briefly to moisten thoroughly.
4. Grease and dust with cornmeal one 2-lb. coffee can or three #2 (20 oz.) cans. Pour batter into cans.
5. Tightly cover the cans with greased foil.
6. Set the cans in a large pot on top of a trivet or baking rack or metal jar lids. Fill the pot with enough boiling water to reach halfway up the cans.
7. Cover the pot and let the bread steam over low heat for 3 hours. (Check sooner if using small cans.)
8. Let the bread cool for 1 hour before removing from cans.

"Life is too short to eat factory-baked bread."
—Doris J. Longacre, *Living More with Less*

OLD MILL SAMPLER

This is my favorite bread recipe, the one I always come back to. It combines cornmeal with whole wheat and rye flours and makes excellent bread, sandwich buns, or even cinnamon raisin bread. You can vary the amount of whole wheat flour you use— less to give a lighter dough, well suited for sandwich buns and cinnamon rolls, or more for a hearty bread.

Yield 3 loaves

2 cups boiling water	**½ cup warm water**
½ cup cornmeal	**¼ cup oil**
¼ cup honey	**½ cup rye flour**
2 tsp. salt	**1-2 cups whole wheat flour**
2 pkgs. dry yeast	**3-4 cups flour**

1. Mix together boiling water, cornmeal, honey, and salt. Cool to lukewarm.
2. Meanwhile, dissolve yeast in warm water.
3. Add oil to cornmeal mixture.
4. Add yeast mixture to lukewarm cornmeal mixture. Mix well.
5. Add rye and wheat flour.
6. Add enough additional flour to make a soft dough.
7. Knead until smooth and elastic, approximately 10 minutes.
8. Place in a greased bowl, turning to grease top. Cover and let rise in warm place until double, approximately 1 hour.
9. Punch down and shape into 3 loaves. Place in greased 8" x 4" pans.
10. Cover and let rise until double, approximately 1 hour.
11. Bake at 375° for 30-35 minutes.

Variation:
Cinnamon Raisin Bread: After the first rising, roll ⅓ of the dough into an 8" x 12" rectangle. Sprinkle the dough with brown sugar, raisins, and cinnamon. Roll up like a jelly roll. Place seam side down in greased pan. Continue with steps 10 and 11.

JANELLE'S MULTI-GRAIN BREAD

For a school project as a sixth grader, my youngest daughter, Janelle, made a poster of different grains, including rye, rice, buckwheat, corn, wheat, millet, oats, and barley. Together we developed a bread recipe using the flours from these grains. The loaves were shared with her classmates and teacher. It was worth an "A."

Yield: 3 medium loaves or 2 large loaves

2 pkgs. dry yeast
½ cup warm water
3 Tbsp. oil
3 Tbsp. honey
2 cups warm water
1 cup instant nonfat dry milk
1 tsp. salt
2 Tbsp. rice flour

2 Tbsp. buckwheat flour
½ cup rye flour
¼ cup cornmeal
¼ cup millet
¼ cup rolled oats
¼ cup barley flour
3½ cups whole wheat flour
2-2½ cups flour

1. Dissolve yeast in ½ cup warm water. Stir and set aside for 5 minutes.
2. In a very large mixing bowl combine oil, honey, 2 cups water, dry milk, salt, rice flour, buckwheat flour, rye flour, cornmeal, millet, rolled oats, and barley flour. Stir well.
3. Add dissolved yeast and whole wheat flour. Beat well.
4. Add enough flour to make a soft dough. Turn onto floured surface and knead for 10-12 minutes.
5. Place in large greased bowl, cover, and set aside to rise in a warm place until double, about 1½ hours.
6. Punch down and shape into loaves (see pages 109-110). Let rise about 30 minutes.
7. Bake at 350° for 40 minutes.
8. Brush tops of loaves with milk to soften crust.

Note: Soy flour may be substituted for the barley and rice flour.

THREE FLOUR BRAIDED BREAD

(Reconciliation Bread)

I have moved many times, lived in many different places, and had neighbors from different cultures and ethnic groups. My life has been enriched by these experiences and persons. But it has not always been without pain, struggle, and effort. For me, this Three Flour Braided Bread has become a symbol of the beauty of unity with diversity that is possible. I call it Reconciliation Bread because three different flour doughs are brought together in harmony—delicious, beautiful harmony.

Yield: 2 braids, or 1 braid and 12 dinner rolls

2½ cups warm water	2 Tbsp. sugar
2 pkgs. dry yeast	1 Tbsp. salt
¼ cup oil	3¼ cups flour

1. Dissolve yeast in 1 cup warm water. Let set 5 minutes.
2. Add oil, sugar, salt, rest of water, and 2¼ cups flour. Beat well.
3. Beat in another cup flour.
4. Divide batter into 3 bowls.
5. To one-third add:

2 Tbsp. molasses	1¼ cups whole wheat flour

To one third add:

2 Tbsp. molasses	1 Tbsp. cocoa *or* carob
1 tsp. caraway seeds	1¼ cups rye flour

To one-third add:

1 cup flour	¼ cup sifted cornmeal

6. Turn each third onto a floured board and knead each dough until smooth and elastic, about 5 minutes.
7. Place in greased individual bowls and let rise about 1 hour.
8. Punch down and divide each dough in half.
9. Roll each piece into a 15" rope.
10. On greased baking sheet braid together a cornmeal, a whole wheat, and a rye rope. Repeat with second set of ropes.

11. Cover and let rise till almost double. It is important not to let loaves rise too long or braids will stretch and separate in baking.
12. Bake at 350° for 30-40 minutes for braided loaves and 15-20 minutes for dinner rolls.

Variation:
Cloverleaf dinner rolls can be made by taking the second half of each dough and dividing it into 12 pieces. Shape each piece into a small round ball and place one ball of each dough (wheat, corn, and rye) into greased muffin pan sections.

Using Leftover Breads

1. Use stale bread to make French toast, bread pudding, stuffing, or bread soufflé.
2. Cut stale bread into attractive shapes, spread with garlic butter and toast at 350° until crisp, usually 10-20 minutes. Use these for dipping in fondue or to float on top of French onion soup.
3. Make croutons by brushing stale bread lightly with oil; then dice them into cubes, sprinkle with seasoned salt, and toast in a slow oven until thoroughly dry and crisp.
4. Leftover bread can be crumbled and added to ground meat dishes as an extender.

ANADAMA BREAD

A tasty cornmeal and molasses yeast bread that keeps well and is grand toasted.

The legend goes that a New England fisherman grew tired of the cornmeal and molasses his wife, Anna, repeatedly made for him. Fed up, he added yeast and wheat to it and baked the first loaf of the bread while muttering, "Anna, d___ her." (Thus the name of the bread.) It's hard to believe that such a good bread was invented by an angry husband.

Yield: 1 loaf

1 cup water	2 Tbsp. oil
1 cup cornmeal	2 tsp. salt
1 pkg. dry yeast	$\frac{1}{3}$ cup soy flour (optional)
1 cup warm water	$2\frac{1}{2}$-$3\frac{1}{2}$ cups whole wheat flour
$\frac{1}{3}$ cup molasses	

1. Boil 1 cup water in a saucepan. Add cornmeal. Cook and stir till thickened. Remove from heat and set aside, covered, to cool slowly. This step can be done the night before.
2. In the morning, or when the cornmeal is approaching room temperature, dissolve the yeast in the warm water.
3. Add molasses, oil, and salt to the cornmeal mixture. Stir to combine till ingredients are blended.
4. Add molasses-cornmeal mixture to the yeast. Stir in the soy flour and 2 cups whole wheat flour.
5. Turn the stiff dough onto a floured surface and knead for 10 minutes, using as much remaining whole wheat flour as needed to keep dough from sticking to hands and surface.
6. Place ball of dough in a greased bowl, turning once to coat surface. Let rise in a warm place, free of drafts, till double in bulk. This will take about 1-1½ hours.
7. Punch down and let rise a second time for about 30 minutes. Shape into a loaf, cover, and let rise till almost double.
8. Bake at 350° for 45-55 minutes.

Note:
This bread may be baked in a 1½- or 2-quart baking dish that has been greased and sprinkled with cornmeal.

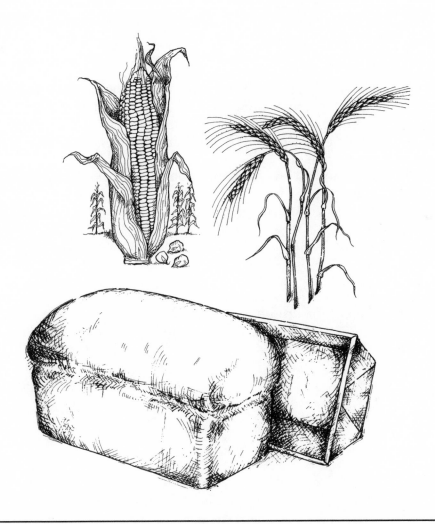

WHEAT RYE OAT BREAD

Yield: 3 loaves

3 cups warm water	3-4 cups flour
1½ pkgs. dry yeast	4 tsp. salt
⅓ cup honey	⅓ cup oil
1 cup instant nonfat dry milk	1½ cups rolled oats
2 cups whole wheat flour	1½ cups rye flour

1. Dissolve the yeast in warm water.
2. Add the honey and dry milk.
3. Stir in the whole wheat flour and 2 cups flour. Beat well with a wooden spoon (100 strokes).
4. Cover and let rise 45 minutes.
5. Fold in the remaining ingredients.
6. Knead on a lightly floured surface, using more flour as needed to keep the dough from sticking. Knead until dough is smooth, approximately 10 minutes.
7. Cover and let rise until double, approximately 1 hour.
8. Punch down.
9. Cover and let rise again until double, approximately 45 minutes.
10. Punch down and shape into 3 loaves. Place in greased 8" x 4" pans.
11. Cover and let rise until double, approximately ½ hour.
12. Bake at 350° for 45 minutes.

"Small quantities of rye flour in bread will improve the texture and aroma of the crumb, give a richer color to the crust, and add a silkiness to the dough, making it easier to work. Its greatest benefit, however, is in increasing the shelf life of the final product."

—Joe Ortiz, *The Village Baker*

PEANUT BUTTER BREAD

The bread for all peanut butter lovers. Try using it for peanut butter and jelly sandwiches.

Yield 2 large loaves

1 medium potato	**½ cup instant nonfat dry milk**
2 cups water	**1 egg**
2 pkgs. dry yeast	**½ cup cornmeal**
¼ cup honey	**2 cups whole wheat flour**
¾ cup creamy peanut butter	**3-4 cups flour**
2 tsp. salt	

1. Peel and cube potato. Cook in 2 cups water until soft.
2. Drain potatoes, reserving the water.
3. Mash the potato.
4. Allow potato water to cool to lukewarm. Add yeast and dissolve.
5. Add mashed potato, honey, peanut butter, salt, dry milk, egg, cornmeal, and whole wheat flour to yeast mixture. Mix well.
6. Add enough additional flour to make a stiff dough.
7. Turn dough onto a floured surface. Knead until smooth and elastic, about 10 minutes.
8. Place in a well greased bowl, turning to grease top. Cover and let rise until double, approximately 1 hour.
9. Punch dough down. Divide in two parts. Shape into loaves and place in greased 9" x 5" pans.
10. Cover and let rise until double, approximately 1 hour.
11. Bake at 375° for 40 minutes.

"Bread is the head of everything."
—An old Ukrainian folk saying

BARLEY LOAF

Yield: 1 loaf

3 Tbsp. barley
1½ cups water
¼ cup warm water
½ tsp. sugar
1 pkg. dry yeast
1 Tbsp. oil
2 Tbsp. honey

½ tsp. salt
1½ cups whole wheat flour
⅓ cup cornmeal
½ cup chopped currants *or* raisins (optional)
1¾-2¼ cups flour

1. Rinse barley in a strainer under cold water. Place barley and 1½ cups water in a saucepan. Cover with a lid and let stand overnight at room temperature.
2. Next day, bring barley and soaking liquid to boiling. Lower heat. Simmer until barley is tender, about 45 minutes. Drain barley and reserve ¾ cup liquid.
3. Whirl barley in blender until smooth. Reserve.
4. Combine warm water and sugar. Sprinkle yeast over water and stir to dissolve. Let stand until bubbly, about 10 minutes.
5. Combine warm barley water, oil, honey, and salt. Add pureed barley. Cool to lukewarm. Stir in yeast mixture.
6. Stir in whole wheat flour, cornmeal, and currants (if desired). Beat in enough flour to make a soft dough.
7. Turn out onto lightly floured surface. Knead until smooth and elastic, about 10 minutes. Use only as much flour as needed to keep dough from sticking.
8. Place in oiled bowl, turning once. Cover and let rise in a warm place, away from drafts, for 1 hour or until double.
9. Punch dough down. Turn out onto lightly floured surface. Knead a few times. Cover dough and let rest 10 minutes.
10. Shape dough into 1 loaf and place in greased 8" x 4" loaf pan. Cover and let rise for 45 minutes, or until double.
11. Bake at 350° for 45 minutes, or until golden brown and loaf sounds hollow when tapped. Remove from pan and cool completely on wire racks.

MULTI-GRAIN BREAD STICKS

Recently, while waiting for our entrees in a New York City restaurant, we were served a basket of delicious, hearty, diagonally sliced bread sticks. I came home and tried to duplicate those bread sticks. The following recipe is the result!

Yield: 4 long thin sticks

2 cups warm whey,
  potato water, *or* water
1 pkg. dry yeast
¼ cup soy grits
2 Tbsp. honey
½ tsp. salt
¼ cup oil

½ cup cornmeal
¼ cup rye flour
1½ cups whole wheat flour
2 Tbsp. flax seeds
1 Tbsp. sesame seeds
2-3 cups flour

1. Dissolve yeast in warm water. Let set for 5 minutes.
2. Add next nine ingredients. Beat well.
3. Add enough flour to make a stiff dough. Turn onto floured surface and knead for 5-8 minutes. Place in a greased bowl, cover, and let rise for 1 hour, or till double in bulk.
4. Punch down and divide into fourths. Roll each piece of dough into a thick, long rope and place on greased cookie sheet.
5. Let rise for 15-20 minutes. Make 4 diagonal gashes across the top of each stick before baking.
6. Bake at 375° for about 20 minutes.

"Warm Water"

What is "warm" when doing yeast-baking? Warm is 105-115°. Above this temperature, the yeast is killed. Below this, the yeast is not properly activated. The temperature of the liquid in which you dissolve the yeast is the most crucial aspect of working with yeast doughs.

MULTI-GRAIN ENGLISH MUFFINS

Yield: 10-12 large muffins

1½ cups warm water	¼ cup cornmeal
1 pkg. dry yeast	¼ cup rye flour
1 Tbsp. honey	¼ cup wheat germ
2 Tbsp. oil	2 cups whole wheat flour
2 tsp. salt	1 cup flour
	or enough to make stiff dough

1. Put 1½ cups warm water in large bowl. Sprinkle in yeast and stir to dissolve.
2. Add honey, oil, salt, cornmeal, rye flour, wheat germ, and whole wheat flour. Stir in enough flour to make a stiff dough.
3. Turn dough onto lightly floured surface and knead 8 to 10 minutes.
4. Place in greased bowl, turning once to grease surface.
5. Cover and let rise till double, about 1¼ hours.
6. Turn onto lightly floured surface. Cover with bowl and let dough rest for 10-15 minutes.
7. On lightly floured surface roll dough to slightly less than ½" thick. Cut with 3" (or 4") round cutter, re-rolling scraps.
8. Dip both sides of each circle in cornmeal. Place circles on cookie sheet. Cover and let rise in warm place until doubled, about 30 minutes.
9. Bake on medium hot ungreased griddle or skillet for 20 minutes, turning every five minutes. An electric skillet works nicely for baking the muffins.
10. Cool thoroughly on wire rack. To serve, insert a fork all around the sides and gently pull them apart into two halves. Toast lightly.

Note: For a puffier muffin, decrease the amount of whole wheat flour and increase the white flour proportionally.

SPREADS

In our childhood home, "spread" generally meant butter. We hand-churned the butter from the rich cream we skimmed from the milk we got from our cows. Our cows all had names. The two I remember most were Babe and Blackie. Babe was the Guernsey and Blackie was the Holstein. Babe gave rich milk with lots of cream. Blackie gave lots of milk but not as much cream.

My brothers and boy cousins who lived next door shared the task of milking by hand. (I tried once but the cow drew up her milk! Or at least that's what they told me.) So my job was "washing up" after the milking. This involved straining the milk through milk filters, putting it into gallon jars which we used for milk storage, and washing up all the milk buckets and equipment.

When we had lots of milk, we used the electric cream separator to separate the cream from the skim milk. Otherwise, we allowed the whole milk to stand in gallon jars until the cream rose to the top of the container. Then we skimmed it off. When we used the electric cream separator, my job of washing up was even more involved, because the cream separator had to be taken apart and carefully cleaned.

We used cream on our cereal, on freshly picked berries, in cooking, and for whipping to make real whipped cream. But we used most of it to make butter. For what seemed like years, we (my brothers, sister, and I) had to churn the cream into butter by hand. One year, we told our parents, "All we want for Christmas is an electric churn!" We got it!

With the electric churn, our only task was to wash the butter. After the cream was churned into butter, we drained the buttermilk from the butter. We saved the buttermilk for recipes that called for it. Or we chilled it and drank it as a beverage. Mom liked it, but we never learned to.

We washed the butter with cold water to remove all the buttermilk, which would spoil quickly. Then we added salt to the butter and, if we were feeling creative, molded the butter into attractive shapes.

As for spreads, jam was second in importance to butter. Our favorite was wild strawberry. Each June we went out to the hayfield to look for little red berries growing on the wild strawberry plants. It seemed to take forever to get enough to make a batch of jam. Our goal was always to pick enough so that Mom could make at least one batch of strawberry jam. All our work was richly rewarded with a thick slice of homemade bread, spread with creamy butter and wild strawberry jam!

Since our childhood days of rich butter and sweet jam, we have learned that too many fats and sweets are not healthy for anyone. So we have tried to learn some new spreads or adapt old ones. We think you'll like our Healthy Butter. If you like butter and a sweet spread, instead of using both, try just small amounts of Honey Butter, a delightful and easy-to-spread combination of butter and honey.

Yogurt is the spread we've learned about since childhood. It is easy to make and versatile. Yogurt is good mixed with fruit and used as a topping for pancakes. Try Yogurt and Applesauce for that. Use Yogurt Cheese plain or mixed with a little honey or peanut butter for a topping on bagels.

Apple butter is one of the traditional spreads from childhood which hasn't changed. It is still delicious, and, if you make it with sweet apples, it doesn't require much sugar. We have included a recipe for Oven Method Apple Butter if you don't have access to the traditional copper kettle.

YOGURT

So simple and so economical, homemade yogurt is also versatile.

Yield: 2 qts.

3 cups instant nonfat dry milk
1 12-oz. can evaporated milk (optional)
6 cups warm water (105°-115°)
⅓ cup yogurt with active culture
(use yogurt from a previous batch or buy fresh plain yogurt)

1. Sterilize all equipment—mixing bowl, spoons, measuring cups, whisk, etc.—by pouring boiling water over it.
2. Combine dry milk, evaporated milk (optional), and water. Stir until well mixed.
3. Add yogurt and stir gently to mix throughout.
4. Pour into sterilized jars.
5. Incubate for 3-6 hours, until yogurt is set. Three good ways to incubate the yogurt are to use a yogurt maker, set jars in an ice chest filled with warm water, or set jars in a warm oven or anywhere that will maintain a temperature of 110°-120° for 3-6 hours.
6. Do not disturb the yogurt while it is setting. However, after about 3 hours and every half hour thereafter, check yogurt to see if it is set.
7. When yogurt is set, place jars in refrigerator. If, for some reason, the yogurt just will not set, you can salvage it by:
    a. Using it in yeast breads and quick breads in place of milk or buttermilk.
    b. Thicken it with plain gelatin—soften 1 pkg. of unflavored gelatin in ¼ cup cold water, warm to dissolve, stir into 1 qt. yogurt. (This yogurt cannot be used for yogurt cheese.)

Variation:
For a sweeter yogurt to be eaten with fruit, or to make a sweet yogurt cheese, add ¼ cup sugar and/or 1 Tbsp. vanilla before incubating.

A little "culture" is a good thing. Yogurt, tart, creamy, and convenient, provides many of the same nutrients as milk. In fact, plain yogurt is the best source of dietary calcium available.

YOGURT CHEESE

Yogurt cheese is a great low-fat, high nutrition substitute for cream cheese or sour cream.

Yield: 2-3 cups

1 qt. yogurt   **cheesecloth**

1. Line a colander with cheesecloth. If the cheesecloth is large mesh, use 2-3 thicknesses.
2. Pour yogurt into cheesecloth-lined colander and allow to drain into a bowl. Save the whey (the liquid drained from the yogurt) for use in bread-baking. The length of time you allow the yogurt to drain determines the consistency of the cheese—the longer the time, the dryer the cheese. If you allow it to drain more than half an hour, put the yogurt and strainer in the refrigerator to avoid food-borne illness.
3. When the consistency you want is reached, use the yogurt cheese or refrigerate it until you need it.

YOGURT AND APPLESAUCE

1 cup yogurt or yogurt cheese
1 cup applesauce

1. Gently mix together, so as not to break the yogurt gel.
2. Serve on pancakes, crepes, or gingerbread.
3. You can also place it in the freezer until frosty crystals form, then serve it as a topping for gingerbread, fruit crisps, cobblers, etc.

PEANUT BUTTER YOGURT

½ cup yogurt
⅓ cup peanut butter (creamy or crunchy)

1. Gently mix together, so as not to break the yogurt gel.
2. Serve on pancakes or waffles. Best when used freshly mixed.

HEALTHY BUTTER

Is butter bad for you? Is margarine better? What about the "trans" fatty acids of hydrogenated oils? How do we cut fat intake to 30% of our calories?

Having grown up milking our own cows, and having had fresh milk, cream, and butter every day, we admit we both like the flavor of real butter. But having studied nutrition, we are also health-conscious. So to bring these seemingly opposite worlds together, we have developed the following compromise. We say compromise because, for health reasons, this spread is not "perfect." It still has saturated fat and cholesterol, although not as much as real butter. It also does not have the "trans" fatty acids of hydrogenated oils.

Yield: 2 cups

1 cup butter   **¼ cup water**
¾ cup oil

1. Bring butter to room temperature. It should be quite soft.
2. Put oil and water in blender. Gradually add butter. Blend until smooth.
3. Place in containers and store in refrigerator.

HONEY BUTTER

A creamy, sweet spread, delicious on hot biscuits, breads, pancakes, muffins, and . . . well almost anything!

Yield: 2 cups

1 cup butter   **1 cup honey**

1. Warm honey slightly. It should flow easily but not be hot.
2. Bring butter to room temperature. It should be quite soft but not melted.
3. In blender, combine honey and butter. Blend until smooth.
4. Place in containers and store in refrigerator.

APPLE BUTTER

Apple butter will always remind me of crisp autumn days, when the competition between the intense, bright, warm sun of summer and the cold, clear air of winter reaches its peak. At this time of year, starting early in the morning, we got out the copper kettle, the cider press, and the apples. With lots of good friends and family, we shared the day making apple butter.

Half the joy of eating apple butter is remembering this day.

30 gallons cider   **oil of cinnamon, and/or cloves,**
5 bushels apples   **and/or red cinnamon**
20-30 lbs. sugar   **candies, as desired**

1. Clean the copper kettle with vinegar and salt until it becomes a bright copper color. Rinse.
2. Set up the copper kettle over a fire ring. Add cider to the kettle. Build a fire.
3. Heat cider to near boiling. Skim off the foam.
4. Continue boiling cider until it has decreased in volume by one-half.

5. Meanwhile, cut the apples into snitz. By "snitz" we mean: peel, core, and cut the apples into quarters or eighths.
6. Gradually add the apple snitz to the cider. Stir constantly. Traditionally, at this time, several copper pennies (they had to be *real* copper pennies) were added to the kettle. As you stirred, you moved these pennies over the bottom of the kettle, thus keeping the apple butter from sticking and burning.
7. Continue cooking and stirring until proper consistency is achieved. This takes most of the day. What is proper consistency? "Until it plops just right." To test: Dip some apple butter out of the kettle and allow to cool. Is it the consistency you like? Stop if it is right. Cook longer if you want it to be thicker.
8. Add sugar and spices to taste.
9. Continue to cook and stir until a slight film forms on the apple butter that you dip out for testing.
10. Can in sterilized pint or quart jars.

Variation:
Mashed pumpkin can be substituted for one-quarter of the apples.

OVEN METHOD APPLE BUTTER

If you are without a copper kettle or don't have enough willing hands, this is an alternative to the previous recipe. However, it is not nearly as much fun. . . or work! On the other hand, you get all the good aroma in your house, and you have a delicious apple butter in less time.

Yield: 6 qts.

5 qts. applesauce
1 cup cider
5-10 cups sugar

2 tsp. cinnamon
1 tsp. cloves (if desired)

1. Combine all ingredients in a greased enamel or glass or stainless steel roasting pan (do not use another metal pan).
2. Bake at 350° for 2-3 hours or until thick. Stir every half hour.

CORNCOB JELLY

This book would be incomplete if we made no reference to corncobs—a side product of the old mill. In the past, before modern corn harvesters, corn was shucked by hand, and the whole corn and cob were brought to the mill. The corn went through a water-powered machine called a corn sheller that removed the corn kernels from the cob. The kernels were then ground into cornmeal. The cobs were collected and used for poultry litter, for starting fires in the woodstoves, and in the famous outhouses. But the best, reddest, cleanest, nicest cobs were used for jelly! This jelly tastes much like apple jelly and has an attractive reddish color.

12 red dried field corncobs
3 pts. water

1. Boil cobs for 1½ hours.
2. Strain the juice.

3 cups of this juice
1 pkg. (⅓ cup) powdered pectin
3 cups sugar

3. Mix juice and pectin together. Bring to a full boil.
4. Add sugar and boil for 1½ minutes.
5. Remove from heat. Skim. Pour into jars and seal.

BREAKFAST and HOLIDAY BREADS

Our usual breakfast bread is toast made from some hearty whole grain bread. It doesn't matter much what kind of bread, just so it is whole grain, toasted, and served with Healthy Butter, Honey Butter, or a homemade jam. However, for Sunday mornings, holidays, special occasions, or guests, we like to prepare special breakfast bread.

We take great pleasure in having those who sleep in our homes waken to the aroma of cinnamon rolls baking. The recipes in this chapter are the ones we use when we want to surprise our families or houseguests with a tempting smell.

First, we offer recipes for fruited breakfast breads, using such fruits as bananas and blueberries. Be sure to try the Banana Buns and Blueberry Sweet Rolls.

Here, too, you will find our family favorites—Caramel Pecan Rolls, Whole Wheat Potato Doughnuts, and Scandinavian Cinnamon Coffee Rolls. These are all yeast doughs which do take a little time and planning, but the rewards in taste and goodwill are worth the effort.

There are occasions when you need something quick and tasty. At those times try Blueberry Coffeecake, Breakfast Puffs, or Gingerbread Doughnuts.

Perhaps calling these "breakfast breads" is an error. When fresh baked goodies are around, we don't wait for breakfast to eat them. Fresh Doughnuts and milk are a favorite after-school snack.

Gingerbread Doughnuts and applesauce make a great dessert.

Finally, we include special holiday breads. These breads take time to make and decorate, but they are a worthy part of our holiday preparation. Decorated, they make gifts that are sure to delight anyone.

Foods, especially breads, are a vital part of our holiday celebrations. At Easter-time we make Hot Cross Buns for Good Friday. For Easter sunrise, we make Easter Nest Coffee Cakes or Orange Bunnies. Among all the other choices we are faced with at Christmas is the matter of which bread to make. Of course, we must have some Christmas Danish, but what else? Shall it be German Stollen or Yogurt Yeast Dough Holiday Cakes? Decisions! Decisions! Sweet decisions!

BREAKFAST PUFFS

You're sure to receive frequent requests for these quick breakfast muffins. I do, especially when all three daughters are home.

Yield: 10-12 muffins

⅓ cup shortening	¼ tsp. salt
⅓ cup sugar	¼ tsp. nutmeg
1 egg	½ cup milk
½ cup whole wheat flour	⅓ cup melted margarine or butter
1 cup flour	cinnamon-sugar mixture
1½ tsp. baking powder	

1. Thoroughly mix shortening, ⅓ cup sugar, and egg.
2. Combine flours, baking powder, salt, and nutmeg.
3. Stir dry ingredients into egg mixture alternately with milk.
4. Fill greased muffin cups ⅔ full.
5. Bake at 350° for 20-25 minutes.
6. Immediately after baking, roll top of puffs in melted margarine, then in cinnamon-sugar mixture. Serve hot.

BANANA BUNS

While bananas are popular in quick breads, they are a delightful surprise in yeast buns. This is the way I most frequently use over-ripe bananas. The heavenly aroma of bananas and cinnamon tempts tasters to partake before these buns have cooled.

Yield: 2 dozen buns

2 pkgs. dry yeast
1 cup warm water
1 cup mashed bananas
$1/3$ cup oil
$1/3$ cup sugar
1 egg

$1/3$ cup instant nonfat dry milk
1 tsp. salt
1 tsp. vanilla
$3^1/2$-4 cups flour
$1^1/2$ cups whole wheat flour

1. Dissolve yeast in water.
2. Combine bananas, oil, sugar, egg, dry milk, salt, and vanilla.
3. Combine dissolved yeast with banana mixture.
4. Add 2 cups flour and mix well.
5. Stir in whole wheat flour and mix well.
6. Add additional flour to make soft dough.
7. Knead on lightly floured surface for 8 minutes.
8. Place in a greased bowl, turning once. Cover and let rise till double.
9. Punch down. Divide dough in half. Cover and let rest 10 minutes.
10. Roll each half into a 16" x 9" rectangle. Spread lightly with softened margarine. Sprinkle each rectangle with half of the following mixture:

$1/2$ cup brown sugar
$1/2$ cup chopped nuts

$1/2$ tsp. allspice
2 tsp. cinnamon

Roll dough up from long side as for jelly roll. Seal seam well.
11. Cut into 12 pieces.
    a. make a cut three-quarters of the way through each piece. Place on greased baking sheet, cut side down, and then fan the sections.

  b. *or* place the cut pieces in a round, square, or
   rectangular-shaped baking pan.

12. Let rise till double.

13. Bake at 350° for 15 minutes for single buns; 20-25 minutes for
   pan buns.

14. Ice with confectioners' sugar icing if desired, *or* drizzle with a
   mixture of 2 cups confectioners' sugar and 2-3 Tbsp. lemon
   juice.

Variation:

After Step #11, these shaped buns can be frozen. Freeze until hard
on baking sheets before removing and placing in airtight plastic
bags. (Freezing before bagging helps them keep their shape and
keeps them from sticking together.)

 When ready to use, remove from freezer. Place on baking
sheets. Allow to thaw and rise, approximately 2-3 hours. Continue
with Steps #13-14.

BLUEBERRY SWEET ROLLS

Yield: 20-24 blueberry rolls

1 pkg. dry yeast	1 cup whole wheat flour
1⅓ cups warm water	3¼-3¾ cups flour
½ cup instant nonfat dry milk	2-3 Tbsp. margarine, softened
¼ cup sugar	½ cup sugar
⅓ cup oil	2 tsp. cinnamon
1 tsp. salt	1 tsp. grated lemon peel
1 egg	2 cups fresh or frozen blueberries, thawed and drained

1. Dissolve yeast in warm water. Let set 5 minutes.
2. Stir in dry milk, sugar, oil, salt, egg, and whole wheat flour. Blend well.
3. Add enough flour to make a moderately stiff dough.
4. Turn onto floured surface and knead for 5 minutes. Place dough in greased bowl, turning once to coat surface.
5. Cover and let rise till double, about 1½ hours.
6. Punch down. Divide in half. Cover and let rest 10 minutes.
7. On floured surface, roll each half into a 14" x 8" rectangle. Spread lightly with softened margarine. Combine ½ cup sugar, cinnamon, and lemon peel. Sprinkle atop dough. Top with blueberries. Press berries lightly into dough. Roll up jelly-roll fashion, starting with long side. Seal edge.
8. Cut each roll into 12 slices. Place cut side down in greased round, square, or rectangular-shaped baking pans. Cover and let rise till double, about 30 minutes.
9. Bake at 375° for 20-25 minutes. While rolls are still warm, top with a thin confectioners' sugar glaze.

Cutting Rolls Trick

Place a piece of regular or heavy-duty sewing thread under the rolled dough where you want to cut, and pull up around sides. Then, crisscross thread across top of roll and pull quickly as though tying a knot.

BLUEBERRY COFFEE CAKE

If you don't have time to make a yeast dough, here is a quick cake-like breakfast treat. It is delicious hot from the oven with a cup of hot chocolate.

Yield: 1 8" pan

Cake:
- ½ cup whole wheat flour
- ½ cup flour
- ½ tsp. salt
- 1 tsp. baking powder
- ¼ tsp. baking soda
- ⅓ cup sugar
- ¼ cup oil
- 1 egg
- ½ cup milk
- 1½ cups blueberries, fresh or frozen, thawed and drained

Topping:
- ⅓ cup whole wheat flour
- ⅓ cup sugar
- ⅓ cup nuts
- 1 tsp. cinnamon
- 2 Tbsp. margarine

1. Mix together all ingredients for the cake except blueberries. Blend until smooth.
2. Pour into greased 8" square pan.
3. Sprinkle batter with blueberries.
4. Mix topping ingredients: whole wheat flour, sugar, nuts, and cinnamon. Cut in the margarine.
5. Sprinkle topping over blueberries.
6. Bake at 375° for 30 minutes.

WHOLE WHEAT COFFEE CAKE

I like to measure all the dry ingredients and make the topping the night before. In the morning as soon as I get up, I mix the batter and let the cake bake while I am getting ready for the day. At breakfast time we have a delicious hot coffee cake, fresh from the oven.

Yield: 1 9" square pan

Cake:

3/4 cup whole wheat flour
3/4 cup flour
3/4 cup sugar
2 1/2 tsp. baking powder

3/4 tsp. salt
1/4 cup shortening
3/4 cup milk
1 egg

Topping:

1/2 cup brown sugar
1/2 cup chopped nuts

2 tsp. cinnamon
2 Tbsp. melted margarine

1. Sift together dry ingredients.
2. Add shortening, milk, and egg. Mix well.
3. Spread half of batter in a greased 9" square pan.
4. Combine topping ingredients and sprinkle half of topping over the batter. Spread remaining batter over this and sprinkle the remaining topping over all.
5. Bake at 350° for 25-30 minutes.

SCANDINAVIAN CINNAMON COFFEE ROLLS

With all the margarine and the egg yolks, this is not a heart healthy treat, but it won my husband's heart! I got this recipe from his mother because it was a family favorite. I made my first batch of the rolls to take on our honeymoon. We are still enjoying this recipe—and our marriage—30 years later.

Yield: 24 rolls

¼ cup sugar
3 cups flour
1 cup whole wheat flour
⅓ cup instant nonfat dry milk
1 tsp. salt

1 cup margarine
1 pkg. dry yeast
1¼ cups warm water
3 egg yolks

1. Combine sugar, flour, whole wheat flour, dry milk, and salt.
2. Cut margarine into above flour mixture.
3. Dissolve yeast in 1¼ cups warm water.
4. Add egg yolks and dissolved yeast to flour/margarine mixture.
5. Beat well. Chill in covered container in refrigerator overnight.
6. Roll half of chilled dough into rectangle, about 12" x 6."
7. Brush with melted margarine. Sprinkle with mixture of sugar and cinnamon. Roll up as jelly roll from long side. Cut roll into 12 1"-slices. Place in greased muffin cups. Repeat with other half of dough.
8. Cover dough in muffin cups. Let rise in warm place about 1 hour. (At this point, you can cover lightly with plastic wrap and refrigerate for 12 hours. When ready to bake, uncover, and allow to set at room temperature for 15 minutes.)
9. Bake at 375° for 15 minutes.
10. Remove from pans and frost with confectioners' sugar icing while still warm.

Variations:
1. Replace 3 egg yolks with 2 eggs.
2. Add 1 tsp. grated lemon rind to the dry ingredients.

CARAMEL PECAN ROLLS

A sweet gooey topping runs down over and through these rolls when the pan is inverted after baking, giving these rolls their nickname, "Sticky Buns." After the last bite, you'll still have treasured memories of finger-licking goodness to enjoy.

Yield: 12 servings

1 pkg. dry yeast	2 Tbsp. oil
1 cup warm water	1 egg
1/3 cup instant nonfat dry milk	1 1/2 cups whole wheat flour
1/4 cup sugar	2 cups flour
1 tsp. salt	

1. Dissolve yeast in warm water.
2. Stir in dry milk, sugar, salt, oil, egg, and whole wheat flour. Beat until smooth.
3. Add enough flour to make a dough that is easy to handle.
4. Place in greased bowl, turning once to grease top. Cover tightly. Refrigerate overnight, or up to 4-5 days.
5. Combine following topping ingredients in saucepan and heat until sugar is dissolved:

1/2 cup brown sugar	1 Tbsp. corn syrup
2 Tbsp. melted margarine	2 Tbsp. water

6. Pour topping into 13" x 9" pan. Sprinkle with:

2/3 cup chopped pecans

7. On floured board, roll dough into 12" x 9" rectangle. Spread with softened margarine and sprinkle with a mixture of the following:

1/3 cup brown sugar	1 Tbsp. cinnamon

8. Roll up tightly, beginning at wide side. Seal edge well. Cut into 1" slices and place in prepared pan with cut side up.

9. Cover and let rise in warm place until double, about 1¹/₂ hours.
10. Bake at 350° for 25-30 minutes.
11. Cool 1-2 minutes. Then invert pan on foil or waxed paper and remove pan.

Variation:

After Step #8, cover tightly with plastic wrap.

Refrigerate 2 to 24 hours. When ready to bake, remove from refrigerator. Uncover dough. Let stand 10 minutes at room temperature. Proceed with steps #10 & #11, except bake at 375°.

"Kneading by Hand"

I know there are food processors, bread machines, and mixers with dough hooks that can eliminate kneading by hand. But for me there is a special magic in a bread's taste and texture when it is kneaded by hand. It cannot be matched by any machine. Maybe it is the warmth of the human hand; maybe it is the sensitivity of an experienced hand nurturing the bread to perfect texture. Knead by hand. You'll taste and feel the difference.

CINNAMON RAISIN TWIST COFFEE CAKE

A yeast coffee cake that rises overnight in the refrigerator and is ready for breakfast or a coffee break in 30-45 minutes.

Yield: 2 9" square cakes

2 pkgs. dry yeast
1²/₃ cups warm water
4-5 cups flour
¹/₂ cup sugar
1¹/₂ tsp. salt

¹/₂ cup instant nonfat dry milk
¹/₄ cup oil
2 eggs
1 cup whole wheat flour
³/₄ cup raisins

1. Dissolve yeast in water. Let stand 5 minutes.
2. Add 2 cups flour, sugar, salt, dry milk, and oil. Beat for 2 minutes.
3. Add eggs and whole wheat flour. Beat vigorously for 2 minutes.
4. Stir in raisins and enough additional flour to make a stiff dough.
5. Turn out onto lightly floured board. Knead until smooth and elastic, about 8-10 minutes. Cover first with plastic wrap, and then a towel. Let rest 20 minutes.
6. Divide dough in half. Roll each half into 12" square. Brush with melted margarine.
7. Combine:
   ¹/₂ cup sugar and 1 Tbsp. cinnamon.
8. Sprinkle center third of each square with sugar mixture. Fold one-third of dough over center third. Sprinkle with sugar mixture. Fold remaining third of dough over the two layers. Cut into strips about 1" wide. Take hold of each end of strip and twist in opposite directions. Seal ends firmly.
   Arrange in 2 greased 9" square pans. Make 2 rows of 6 twists side by side in each pan. Brush lightly with oil, then cover loosely with plastic wrap. Refrigerate 2-24 hours.
9. When ready to bake, remove from refrigerator. Uncover dough carefully. Let stand at room temperature for 10 minutes.
10. Bake at 375° for 30 minutes or until done. Remove from pans and cool on wire racks. Drizzle with confectioners' sugar icing, if desired.

HONEY-DIPPED WHOLE WHEAT DOUGHNUTS

These easy-to-do-doughnuts require no shaping and are a big hit with young people. Make up the dough ahead and let them do the frying. Be sure to follow safety precautions around hot oil.

Yield: 3¹/₂ dozen

Dip:

²/₃ **cup honey**	¹/₃ **cup water**

Combine honey and water. Heat gently, stirring until well blended. Chill several hours.

Dough:

1¹/₄ **cups warm water**	2 **eggs**
1 **pkg. dry yeast**	2 **Tbsp. oil**
3 **Tbsp. sugar**	1 **cup whole wheat flour**
1 **tsp. salt**	2¹/₂ **cups flour**
¹/₃ **cup instant nonfat dry milk**	

1. Dissolve yeast in warm water. Let set 5 minutes.
2. To dissolved yeast add sugar, salt, dry milk, eggs, oil, and whole wheat flour. Beat well.
3. Add enough flour to make a stiff batter. Cover bowl. Let rise in a warm place until double in bulk, about 1 hour.
4. Stir batter down. Drop by rounded teaspoonfuls into hot oil, 365°. Fry a few at a time until golden brown, about 2 minutes on each side. (Fat that is too hot can cause over-browning before the insides get done. Lower temperatures allow the doughnuts to absorb oil before they are brown on the outside.)
5. Drain on absorbent paper about 1 minute. Then immerse fried doughnuts into chilled honey mixture. Serve immediately.

Variations:

1. Roll honey-dipped doughnuts in chopped nuts.

2. Omit honey dip and shake in confectioners' sugar or a cinnamon sugar mixture.

WHOLE WHEAT POTATO DOUGHNUTS

Don't expect to eat just one!

Yield: 2 dozen large doughnuts

1 cup warm mashed potatoes	**½ cup oil**
½ cup sugar	**1½ cups warm water**
2 pkgs. dry yeast	**2 eggs**
2 tsp. salt	**2 cups whole wheat flour**
2 tsp. vanilla	**4-5 cups flour**
⅓ cup instant nonfat dry milk	

1. Combine mashed potatoes, sugar, yeast, salt, vanilla, dry milk, oil, and warm water. Stir well. Let stand for 30 minutes, or till slightly foamy.
2. Add eggs, whole wheat flour, and enough of the flour to make a soft dough.
3. Turn out onto lightly floured surface. Knead until smooth, about 5 minutes.
4. Place dough in greased bowl, turning once to grease surface.
5. Cover. Let rise in warm place till double, about 45 minutes.
6. Punch down and turn out on lightly floured surface. Roll to ½" thickness. Cut with 3" cutter. Place on floured baking sheets, cover, and let rise till almost double, about 30 minutes.
7. Fry in deep hot fat (365°). Drain on absorbent paper.
8. Serving options:
   a. Put warm, not hot, doughnut in a paper or plastic bag with confectioners' sugar. Shake to coat.
   b. Coat with mixture of cinnamon and sugar.
   c. Ice with chocolate frosting.
   d. Dip hot doughnuts into one of the following glazes:

Orange Glaze:
Stir together 2 cups confectioners' sugar, ¼ cup orange juice, and 1 tsp. finely grated orange rind (optional) until smooth. Dip tops of doughnuts in glaze while warm.

Sugar Glaze:
Dissolve 2 tsp. unflavored gelatin in ⅓ cup hot water. Add 1 lb. confectioners' sugar, 2 tsp. vanilla, and 2 tsp. melted butter. Mix well. Dip warm doughnuts in glaze and allow to drain.

Daisy Alderfer, a grandmotherly figure from our childhood, won our hearts with her potato doughnuts, but her recipe left something to be desired. After listing ingredients the recipe only says: "proceed according to common sense." Since that time we have learned a few hints that you might find helpful.

Greaseless doughnuts:
Add 1 Tbsp. vinegar or 1 tsp. ginger to oil before heating. This prevents the dough from absorbing too much grease while frying.

Glazing hint:
Hang glazed doughnuts on a wooden dowel over a clean dishpan. Allow the doughnuts to drip dry.

Doughnut Hole Sticky Muffins:
Grease 12 muffin pan cups. In the bottom of each cup place 1 Tbsp. brown sugar, 1 tsp. light corn syrup, ½ tsp. water, and 1 tsp. chopped nuts. Arrange 4 doughnut holes in each cup. Cover with a cloth and let rise until double. Bake at 350° for about 20-25 minutes. Carefully invert pan as soon as they come out of the oven.

Baked doughnuts:
Cut dough with a doughnut cutter that has a large hole. Place on greased cookie sheets and let rise until light. Bake at 375° until delicately brown, about 12-15 minutes. Brush with butter on all sides while still warm and roll in granulated sugar cinnamon mixture.

GINGERBREAD DOUGHNUTS

For a new twist, shape this gingerbread dough into spirals for an unbeatable quick doughnut.

Yield: 18 doughnuts

2 cups flour	2 eggs
1 cup whole wheat flour	$\frac{1}{3}$ cup brown sugar
1 Tbsp. baking powder	$\frac{1}{2}$ cup yogurt
2 tsp. ginger	$\frac{1}{4}$ cup light molasses
$\frac{1}{2}$ tsp. baking soda	$\frac{1}{4}$ cup oil
$\frac{1}{2}$ tsp. salt	cooking oil for deep frying

1. Stir together flours, baking powder, ginger, baking soda, and salt.
2. Beat eggs till thick and lemon-colored.
3. Beat in brown sugar, yogurt, molasses, and $\frac{1}{4}$ cup oil.
4. Stir in dry ingredients just until moistened. Let dough rest 15 minutes. Turn dough onto floured surface and knead for half a minute.
5. Flatten dough on lightly floured surface to 9" square, about $\frac{3}{4}$" thick. (Unlike a yeast dough, this batter does not hold together well. Handle dough as little as possible.)
6. Begin heating oil to 365°.
7. To shape these doughnut twists, cut into 9 strips 1" wide. Cut each strip in half crosswise, making 18 $4\frac{1}{2}$" strips. Gently roll strips of dough into 9" ropes. Fold in half. Take hold of each end of strip and twist in opposite directions. Seal ends together firmly.
8. As soon as shaped, fry in deep hot oil (365°) about 2 to 3 minutes, or till done. Drain on absorbent paper.
9. Brush warm doughnuts with Lemon Glaze: Combine and stir till smooth.

2 cups sifted confectioners' sugar	$\frac{1}{2}$ tsp. grated lemon peel
2 Tbsp. milk	1 Tbsp. lemon juice

10. Best served fresh.

EASTER NEST COFFEE CAKE

Too pretty to eat but too delectable not to.

Yield: 1 coffee cake

1 pkg. dry yeast
³/₄ cup warm water
¹/₄ cup sugar
3 Tbsp. instant nonfat
   dry milk

¹/₄ cup oil *or* margarine
1 tsp. salt
1 egg
1 cup whole wheat flour
2-2¹/₂ cups flour

1. Dissolve yeast in warm water. Let set for 5 minutes.
2. Add sugar, dry milk, oil or margarine, salt, egg, and whole wheat flour.
3. Add enough flour to make a soft dough.
4. On floured surface, knead 8-10 minutes, till smooth and elastic.
5. Place in greased bowl, turning once to grease surface.
6. Cover. Let rise in warm place till double, about 1 hour.
7. Punch down. Divide in thirds. Cover. Let rest 10 minutes.
8. Shape ¹/₃ of dough into 6 "eggs." Place close together in the center of greased baking sheet. For nest, shape remaining dough in two 26" ropes. Twist together. Coil around "eggs." Seal ends.
9. Cover. Let rise till double, about 45-60 minutes.
10. Bake at 375° for 15-20 minutes.
11. Frost coffee cake with confectioners' sugar icing, starting with "eggs." As soon as iced, sprinkle with candy decorations. Ice coiled "nest." Sprinkle with coconut that has been tinted green with a few drops of green food coloring.

Variation:

If you want to make two smaller coffee cakes, simply divide dough in half after punching down in #7. Divide each half into thirds and proceed as instructed.

ORANGE BUNNIES

Fun to make. The whole family will want to help shape these irresistible bunnies.

Yield: 24 bunnies

1 pkg. dry yeast	**2 cups whole wheat flour**
1¼ cups warm water	**2 beaten eggs**
⅓ cup instant nonfat dry milk	**¼ cup orange juice**
¼ cup sugar	**2 Tbsp. grated orange peel**
⅓ cup oil or margarine	**3¼-3¾ cups flour**
1 tsp. salt	

1. Soften yeast in warm water. Let stand 5 minutes.
2. Add dry milk, sugar, oil or margarine, salt, and whole wheat flour. Beat well.
3. Add eggs, orange juice, peel, and enough flour to make a soft dough.
4. Turn out on a lightly floured surface and knead till smooth and elastic, about 8 minutes.
5. Place dough in a lightly greased bowl, turning once to grease surface. Cover and let rise till double, about 2 hours.
6. Punch down. Cover and let rest 10 minutes.
7. To shape: On lightly floured surface roll dough into rectangle ½" thick. Cut dough in strips about ½" wide, and roll between hands to smooth. Shape into bunnies.

For twist bunnies:

For each, you'll need a 14" strip of dough. On lightly greased baking sheet, lap one end of strip over other to form a loop.

Bring end that's underneath up over top end, letting one end extend on each side to make ears. Pat tips of ears to shape in a point. Roll small ball of dough for tail; place atop dough at bottom of loop.

For curlicue bunnies:

For each, you'll need a 15" strip of dough. On lightly greased baking sheet, coil ⅔ of the strip loosely in one direction for the body and coil the other third of the strip in the opposite direction for the head. For ears, pinch off ½" strips and roll between hands till smooth. Let point make tip of ear. Snip off opposite end and place ear next to head. Pinch off a bit of dough and roll into a ball for tail.

8. After shaping, cover. Let rise till nearly double, about 45-60 minutes. Bake at 375° 12-15 minutes. While warm, brush with Sugar Glaze, page 151.

Variations:
Orange Bowknot Rolls:
Follow the above recipe through Step #6. Then roll dough into an 18" x 10" rectangle, ½" thick. Cut strips 10" long and ¾" wide. Roll each strip back and forth lightly under your fingers. Loosely tie dough strip into a knot. Place on greased baking sheet. Proceed as in Step #8. If desired, ice with Orange Glaze (page 150). Makes 24 bowknot rolls.

Orange Birdies:
After making an Orange Bowknot as in the variation above, place one end of knot up and one end down. Shape top end into head and beak. Flatten bottom end and snip with scissors to form tail. Place on greased baking sheet. Proceed as in Step # 8. When cool, decorate with colored icing.

Orange Swirls:
Follow the Orange Bunnies recipe through Step #6. Divide dough in half. Roll each half into a 12" x 9" rectangle, ¼" thick. Spread lightly with softened margarine. Sprinkle with the following:

Orange Filling:
| ½ cup brown sugar | 1 Tbsp. grated orange peel |
| ½ cup chopped walnuts | |

Beginning at wide edge, roll each rectangle as a jelly roll. Seal edges. Cut into 1" slices. Place cut side down on greased baking pans. Proceed as in Step #8. Makes 24 rolls.

HOT CROSS BUNS

These buns, made with 100% whole wheat flour, dried fruit, nuts, and honey, are very dense, hardy, and earthy—perfect for Good Friday.

Yield: 30 buns

1 cup raisins
1 cup dried currants
1 cup dried apricots
1 cup walnuts, chopped
1 pkg. dry yeast
½ cup warm water
6 cups whole wheat flour
2 tsp. salt

2 large eggs, beaten
  (some set aside)
3 Tbsp. honey
1 cup very hot water
1 cup cold buttermilk
more water as required
¼ cup butter, room
  temperature

1. Chop raisins. Steam the raisins and currants briefly, drain and cool. Chop and steam the apricots so that they are about as soft as the raisins. Toast the nuts lightly.
2. Dissolve yeast in warm water and set aside.
3. Mix the flour and salt in a bowl, making a well in the center.
4. Beat the eggs slightly in a small bowl. Reserve about 3 tablespoons to use for egg wash later.
5. In a separate bowl, mix the honey and hot water. Add the buttermilk. Stir in the beaten eggs.
6. Pour the liquids and the yeast into the well in the flour and mix; then knead. Keep your hands wet as you work the stiff, sticky dough, letting it take in as much water as it requires to become soft and supple. When the dough is silky and elastic, add the butter in the French manner by smearing it on the countertop and kneading until all the butter has been incorporated. Gently knead in the fruits and nuts a handful at a time.
7. Shape dough into a ball and place in a bowl. Cover and let rise in a warm place for about 1½ hours. It may rise more slowly than you expect because of the weight of the rich ingredients, so be prepared to give it a little extra time. When a hole poked about ½" deep in the center of the dough does not fill in at all, the dough is ready to deflate.

8. Punch down and carefully shape into a smooth round ball again. Let the dough rise once more. The second rising time will be about half as long as the first.

9. Shape the dough into 30 smooth balls and arrange them 3 down and 5 across on 2 12" x 18" greased cookie sheets that have been dusted with mixture of 1 Tbsp. cinnamon, ½ tsp. nutmeg, ¼ tsp. cloves, plus a dash of cardamom and ginger. After shaping, allow the dough to relax about 10 minutes, and then flatten the balls slightly with your palm.

10. Let buns rise in warm place for a half hour or more. Make the egg wash by combining the reserved egg plus 1½ Tbsp. water. Beat until smooth. Just before the buns are ready to go in the oven, use a spatula to mark each bun with an indented cross, pressing down about halfway into the dough. Brush with egg wash. Let dough recover for a few minutes.

11. Bake at 375° for 15-20 minutes. Check to make sure the buns are not burning on the bottom. If necessary, move the baking sheets around in the oven to insure an even bake.

12. After they cool, use a confectioners' sugar frosting to make a cross on the top of each bun. The buns are splendid when re-warmed.

I prefer dried fruits to candied fruits because their color and flavor are more natural. If dried fruits are very dry, they will pull moisture out of the bread. To soften them, cover the fruit with boiling water. Let set for 10-15 minutes. Drain and gently squeeze the fruit before adding it to the dough. The drained, sweet flavored liquid can be used as the liquid in the recipe.

SWEDISH SAINT LUCIA BUNS

December 13 is St. Lucia's Day. She was a young Christian martyr who died in 303 A.D. In Sweden, she is the Queen of Lights. By tradition, on this day the oldest daughter in a Swedish family, wearing a long white robe and a crown of greens and seven candles, wakes up members of the family to serve them a light breakfast of coffee and saffron buns.

Yield: 18 buns

½-1 tsp. saffron threads	1 tsp. salt
¼ cup boiling water	1 egg
1¼ cups warm water	1 cup whole wheat flour
⅓ cup sugar	3-4 cups flour
2 pkgs. dry yeast	1 egg
⅓ cup instant nonfat dry milk	1 tsp. water
¼ cup oil	18 raisins

1. Soak saffron in boiling water and set aside.
2. Combine warm water and 1 tsp. sugar. Sprinkle with yeast. Stir to dissolve. Set aside for 5 minutes.
3. Add dry milk, remaining sugar, oil, salt, egg, saffron, and saffron water.
4. Gradually add 1 cup whole wheat flour and 1 cup white flour. Beat vigorously.
5. Add enough flour to make a soft dough. Turn dough out onto lightly floured surface and knead 8 to 10 minutes.
6. Place in a greased bowl, turning to grease top. Cover and let rise in a warm place until doubled in bulk, about 1 hour.
7. Punch dough down. Divide into 18 pieces. Roll each piece of dough into a 10" long strip. Curl ends in opposite directions, forming "S" shapes.
8. Place on greased baking sheets. Cover and let rise in warm place until doubled in size, about 20-30 minutes. Brush with 1 egg beaten with 1 tsp. water. Press a dark raisin deep into center of each coil. Bake at 350° for 15 minutes. Cool on wire racks. Cover buns with cloth towel to retain softness.

HOLIDAY SWEET BREAD

Yield: 2 9" or 10" round pans of rolls

1 cup warm water
2 pkgs. dry yeast
⅓ cup instant nonfat dry milk
½ cup butter *or* margarine,
  softened
⅔ cup sugar

½ tsp. salt
3 eggs
2 cups whole wheat flour
½ cup mashed potatoes
3-3½ cups flour

1. Dissolve yeast in warm water.
2. Add dry milk, butter, sugar, salt, eggs, whole wheat flour, and mashed potatoes to yeast mixture. Beat well.
3. Stir in enough flour to make a moderately stiff dough.
4. Turn out on floured surface. Knead 8-10 minutes, till smooth and elastic. Place in greased bowl, turning once to grease surface. Cover. Let rise till double, about 1½ hours.
5. Punch down. Divide dough into 2 parts. Cover and let rest 10 minutes.
6. Shape each part into 8 equal balls. Place in greased 9" or 10" round baking pan. Let rise till light, about 45 minutes.
7. Bake at 350° for 25-30 minutes. Remove from pans. Cool.

"For when we smell bread baking, it's simple: we know, as people have known for thousands of years, that all is well, that soon we will eat, and eat well. We know we are home."
—Crescent Dragonwagon, *Dairy Hollow House Soup and Bread*

CHRISTMAS DANISH SWIRLS

This flaky pastry is everything but fat-free. But once a year we indulge. Decorated with red and green sprinkles, this is a festive breakfast bread for Christmas morning.

Yield: 24 swirls

2½-3 cups flour
½ cup sugar
1½ tsp. salt
2 Tbsp. cornstarch
2 tsp. grated lemon peel
⅓ cup instant nonfat dry milk
2 pkgs. yeast
1¼ cups very warm water

¼ cup oil *or* margarine
2 eggs (at room temperature), separated
1 cup whole wheat flour
1½ cups (3 sticks) margarine
1 Tbsp. water
confectioners' sugar frosting
red and green sprinkles

1. Mix 1 cup flour, sugar, salt, cornstarch, lemon peel, dry milk, and undissolved yeast in a large bowl.
2. Gradually add very warm water and oil to dry ingredients and beat 2 minutes, scraping bowl occasionally. Add 2 egg yolks, 1 egg white (reserve remaining egg white), and 1 cup whole wheat flour. Beat vigorously by hand or with electric mixer on high for 2 minutes, scraping bowl occasionally. Add enough additional flour to make a stiff batter. Stir just until blended. Cover tightly with aluminum foil. Chill about l hour.
3. Spread 1½ cups margarine into a 10" x 12" rectangle on waxed paper. Chill 1 hour.
4. Roll chilled dough into a 12" x 16" rectangle on a lightly floured surface. Place margarine slab on ⅔ of dough. Fold uncovered third over middle section. Cover with remaining third. Give dough a quarter turn. Roll into a 12" x 16" rectangle. Fold as above. Turn, roll, and fold once more. Chill 1 hour. Repeat procedure of 2 rollings, foldings, turnings, and chillings two more times. Then refrigerate overnight in a covered plastic container or floured plastic bag.
5. Divide dough in half. On a lightly floured board roll half the dough into a 15" x 6" rectangle. Cut 12 strips, 15" x ½." Twist

each strip and form into a swirl, sealing ends well. Place on greased baking sheets. Repeat with remaining piece of dough. Cover lightly with plastic wrap. Refrigerate overnight.

6. Combine reserved egg white with 1 Tbsp. water. Brush rolls with egg white mixture.

7. Bake at 375° about 15 to 20 minutes, or until done. Remove from baking sheets and cool on wire racks. Frost with confectioners' sugar frosting and decorate with sprinkles.

YOGURT YEAST DOUGH

Use for candy canes, Christmas trees, and Christmas wreaths.

Yield: 3 Christmas coffee cakes

2 cups yogurt
2 pkgs. dry yeast
½ cup warm water
¼ cup oil *or* margarine
⅓ cup sugar

2 tsp. salt
2 eggs
2 cups whole wheat flour
4-5 cups flour

1. Heat yogurt over low heat just until lukewarm.
2. Dissolve yeast in warm water in large mixing bowl.
3. Add oil or margarine, sugar, salt, eggs, whole wheat flour, and warm yogurt. Beat until well combined.
4. Stir in remaining flour as needed until dough cleans side of bowl.
5. Knead dough on well-floured board until smooth, approximately 10 minutes. Place in greased bowl, turning once to bring greased side up. Cover. Let rise in warm place about 1 hour, or until dough is double. Punch down. Shape as desired (see below). Bake at 375° for 15-20 minutes. Frost and decorate.

Shaping Ideas (Divide dough into thirds.)
Christmas Tree:
Roll one-third of dough out as a rectangle 15" x 6," and spread lightly with margarine. Sprinkle with cinnamon, sugar, nuts, and/or raisins. Roll up jelly-roll fashion and cut into 11 sections. Place on a greased cookie sheet, cut side down in an arrangement to represent a Christmas tree.

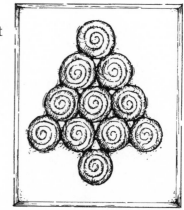

Christmas Wreath:
Roll another one-third of dough as above, but do not cut into sections. Instead, join ends making a circle. Cut three-fourths of the way through the dough at 1" intervals. Lay cut sections on side.

Christmas Candy Cane:

Roll another one-third of dough out as a rectangle 15" x 6."
Down center third of dough sprinkle a mixture of your choice
of nuts, dried apricots, dates, raisins, cinnamon and sugar.
Make cuts 2" deep from outer edge of long sides at ½" intervals
with knife. Crisscross strips over filling. Place on greased
cookie sheet, stretching and curving dough to form cane.

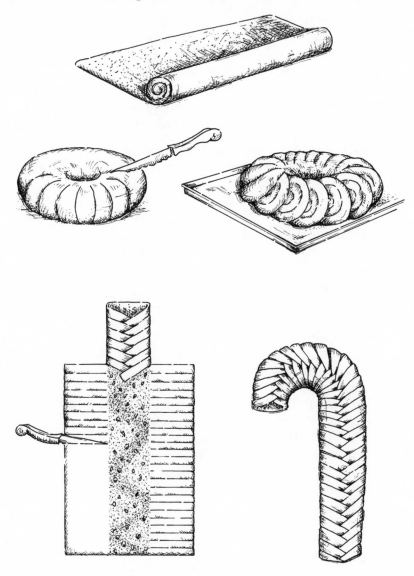

GERMAN STOLLEN

Sweet, evenly textured, flecked with nuts and fruits, and decorated attractively, this is one of the most delicious holiday breads.

Yield: 2 large oval stollens

4-5 cups flour
$\frac{1}{2}$ cup sugar
1 tsp. salt
2 pkgs. dry yeast
$\frac{3}{4}$ cup milk
$\frac{1}{2}$ cup water
$\frac{2}{3}$ cup margarine

3 eggs
1$\frac{1}{2}$ cups whole wheat flour
$\frac{3}{4}$ cup chopped, blanched almonds
$\frac{3}{4}$ cup mixed dried fruits *or* dates
$\frac{1}{3}$ cup golden seedless raisins
confectioners' sugar frosting

1. Mix 2 cups flour, sugar, salt, and undissolved yeast.
2. Combine milk, water, and margarine in a saucepan. Heat over low heat until liquids are warm.
3. Gradually add to dry ingredients and beat 2 minutes, scraping bowl occasionally. Add eggs and whole wheat flour. Beat vigorously for 2 minutes.
4. Stir in enough additional flour to make a soft dough. Turn out onto lightly floured board. Knead about 8 to 10 minutes, until smooth and elastic.
5. Place in greased bowl, turning to grease top. Cover. Let rise in warm place until doubled in bulk, about 1$\frac{1}{2}$ hours.
6. Combine almonds, candied fruits and/or dates, and raisins.
7. Punch dough down. Turn out onto lightly floured board. Knead in nut and fruit mixture.
8. Divide dough into 3 pieces. Roll each piece of dough into a 12" x 7" oval. Fold in half lengthwise. Place on greased baking sheets. Cover. Let rise in warm place, free from draft, until doubled in bulk, about 45 minutes.
9. Bake at 350° for 20 to 25 minutes, or until done. Remove from baking sheets and cool on wire racks. Frost with confectioners' sugar frosting while warm. If desired, decorate with blanched almonds and candied cherries.

Note: These breads freeze well. However, wait to frost and decorate until ready to serve.

FUNNY CAKE PIE

There are times when I'm not sure if a recipe came from my Pennsylvania Dutch heritage or from my life in Appalachia. This recipe definitely comes from my Pennsylvania Dutch heritage.

True to its name, Funny Cake Pie is a cake baked in a pie crust, with a surprise layer between the cake and the pie crust.

We usually eat this as a breakfast sweet or for coffee break.

Yield: 1 9" pie

1 9" unbaked whole wheat pie crust

Sauce:
3 Tbsp. carob *or* cocoa powder **3 Tbsp. margarine**
½ cup water **1 tsp. vanilla**
⅔ cup sugar

Cake:
½ cup whole wheat flour **¼ cup oil**
¾ cup flour **1 tsp. vanilla**
1¼ tsp. baking powder **1 egg**
½ tsp. salt **½ cup milk**
¾ cup sugar

Topping:
2-3 Tbsp. chopped nuts and/or coconut (optional)

1. Line a 9" pie pan with crust. (See recipe for Pie Crust on page 221.)
2. To make sauce, heat together carob powder, water, and sugar. Stir until sugar is dissolved.
3. Remove from heat and add margarine and vanilla. Stir to melt margarine. Cool slightly.
4. Mix all cake ingredients together and blend until smooth. Pour into pie crust.
5. Pour sauce over cake batter.
6. If desired, top with 2-3 Tbsp. of chopped nuts and/or coconut.
7. Bake at 350° for 50-55 minutes.

BAGELS

A ring-shaped roll with a tough, chewy texture, made from a yeast dough that is dropped briefly into boiling water and then baked.

Yield: 6-8 bagels

$1\frac{1}{2}$ cups warm water
2 Tbsp. honey
1 pkg. dry yeast
2 cups flour
$2\frac{1}{4}$ cups whole wheat flour

$\frac{1}{2}$ tsp. salt
3-4 quarts boiling water
   (do not use softened water)
2 tsp. honey

1. Mix together warm water, 2 Tbsp. honey, and yeast. Let set until bubbly.
2. Add flour, whole wheat flour, and salt. Knead dough for 5-8 minutes.
3. Place dough in greased bowl, cover, and let rise until double, about 45 minutes.
4. Punch down and divide into 6-8 pieces. Shape each piece into a ball. Poke a hole in the center and pull gently to enlarge the hole, working each bagel into a uniform shape. Let rest 5 minutes on a lightly floured surface.
5. Add 2 tsp. honey to 3-4 qts. boiling water. Place bagels, 2 or 3 at a time, in boiling honey water. Adjust the heat so that the water is simmering all the time. After two minutes, turn bagels over and allow to simmer for 2 more minutes.
6. Remove bagels from water with a slotted spoon. Then place them an inch apart on a greased cookie sheet. If desired, brush bagels with a mixture of 1 egg and 1 Tbsp. water for a shiny finish.
7. Bake at 400° for 20 minutes, or until crusty and golden brown. Cool on wire racks.
8. To serve, split and toast. Top with desired spread.

Variations:
After the first rising, and before dividing into 6-8 pieces, knead one of the following into the dough:
Cinnamon-Raisin Bagels—$\frac{1}{2}$ cup raisins and 2 tsp. cinnamon.
Sesame or Poppy Seed Bagels—2 Tbsp. sesame or poppy seeds.
Onion Bagels—3 Tbsp. sautéed, minced onion.

CULTURAL FOODS

We started life with a mix of Pennsylvania Dutch culture, supplied by our parents' heritage, and Appalachian culture, gained from our environment. Added to this was the influence of the many and varied visitors who frequented our home. Our parents had an extensive network of friends, many of whom were mission workers in foreign countries. When these friends came for a visit, Mom would frequently ask them to cook a special meal for us. This meal was to be typical of the country in which they lived, given the constraints of available ethnic foods in our local supermarkets! These were always fun times. We learned early to appreciate a diversity of foods and cultures.

As we grew up and moved out on our own, we began to collect some of these recipes. We have discovered that stone-ground flours lend themselves to many of these cultures' foods, since stone-grinding of whole grains is the most universal preparation of grains.

Our most profound experience of this was grinding corn on stones together with an Indian woman in Guatemala. Though we didn't know a common spoken language, we did share a common food language. While Guatemalan and North American tortillas are made with different kinds of flour, the flour in both cases is stone-ground. Our two tortilla recipes begin this chapter.

As a child, part of the fun we had while eating other cultural foods was that normal table manners didn't apply. We remember sitting on the floor in our living room, eating Indian curry and chapati. We loved eating African injera and wat with our fingers. Don't miss the recipes for Chapati and Injera in this section.

Perhaps less strange are some of the traditional breads from Europe, such as Irish Soda Bread, English Scones, and Italian Bread. It may be that in the foods we eat, we Americans are most truly a melting pot of cultures. May our enjoying these varied foods help us appreciate and safeguard the varied cultures and people they represent.

WHOLE WHEAT TORTILLAS

So simple, so inexpensive, and so quick, why buy commercial tortillas? Children can help roll them out.

Yield: 12 tortillas

1½ cups flour   **1 cup water**
1½ cups whole wheat flour

1. Combine above ingredients.
2. Knead. Dough is stiffer than bread dough.
3. Divide into 12 pieces. Work each ball of dough till pliable.
4. Roll as thin as possible.
5. Cook on very hot ungreased griddle until freckled on one side.
6. Turn and cook on second side.
7. Place between folds of towel to keep pliable.

Bread has two basic ingredients: flour and water. The tortilla of Latin America is the simplest of unleavened breads. A combination of flour and water, shaped by hand and cooked on an ungreased griddle, yields a thin pancake that can be eaten hot or cold, for a meal or a snack. They can be eaten plain or used as a scoop to bring other food to one's mouth.

Filled with meat or beans and topped with chopped tomatoes, lettuce, and grated cheese, tortillas become tacos. I always try to make more tortillas than I need for one meal so that I'll have some for enchiladas, a tortilla filled with meat or beans and cheese and baked topped with a tomato sauce. But in our house, leftover tortillas often get eaten as breakfast burritos, made by spooning scrambled eggs onto a heated tortilla, topping it with cheese and rolling it up. Tostados are yet another way to eat tortillas. The filling is put on top of a flat tortilla that has been baked at 350° for 15 minutes.

TORTILLAS

I raised an open pollinated, flint corn (Indian corn) in my garden this past year. After harvesting, drying, and shelling it, I had my husband grind it at the mill. It made a beautiful corn flour which makes great tortillas!

Yield: 6-10 tortillas

1½ cups flour
¼ cup cornmeal
¼ cup whole wheat flour

1 tsp. salt
¼ cup shortening
½ cup warm water

1. Combine flour, cornmeal, whole wheat flour, and salt.
2. With pastry blender, cut in shortening until particles are very fine.
3. Gradually add warm water to make a stiff dough.
4. On a lightly floured surface, knead until smooth and flecked with air bubbles.
5. Place in a greased container, turning to grease top. Cover tightly and refrigerate 4-24 hours.
6. Return to room temperature.
7. Divide into 6 to 10 pieces. Shape into balls and roll into thin circles. Roll as thin as possible.
8. Bake on a hot ungreased griddle, approximately 20 seconds.
9. Turn and bake on other side.
10. Serve warm.

"In civilized America we no longer had bread; we had something sanitized and puffy that no self-respecting man would want to eat . . . But here in the peasant culture of Mexico there was still bread made from the simple ground wheat of the countryside, filled with impurities and flavor, and when we Americans tasted it after many years of chewing paste, we devoured it like starving pigs."

—James Michener, *Mexico*

INJERA—ETHIOPIAN FLAT BREAD

Injera is an African bread which is thicker than a crepe but thinner than a pancake. Its delicate texture and delightful flavor are good with hot spicy stews such as curry or wat.

Yield: 20 injera

3 cups flour
½ cup whole wheat flour
½ cup cornmeal
1 tsp. salt

3 tsp. baking powder
1 pkg. dry yeast
3½ cups warm water

1. Mix all ingredients together in large bowl.
2. Cover and let set an hour or longer, until batter is quite stretchy. (Dough can be allowed to set for 1-5 hours.)
3. Blend in blender 2 cups batter and ½ cup water. Repeat with remaining batter. Batter will be quite thin.
4. Pour ½ cup batter on a medium hot, non-stick griddle. Quickly swirl pan to spread batter as thinly as possible.
5. Do not turn! It is cooked through when bubbles appear all over top and top appears dry.
6. Lay each injera on a clean towel for a minute or two, then stack in a covered dish to keep warm.
7. Serve warm with a spicy stew.

"I grew up kissing books and bread. In our house, whenever anyone dropped a book or let fall a chapati or a "slice," which was our word for a triangle of buttered leavened bread, the fallen object was required not only to be picked up, but also kissed, by way of apology for a clumsy act of disrespect. I was as careless as any child, and accordingly, during my childhood years, I kissed a large number of "slices" and also my fair share of books . . . Bread and books: food for the body and food for the soul—what could be more worthy of our respect, and even love?"
—Salman Rushdie, *Is Nothing Sacred?*

CHAPATIS

These delicious flat breads from India are good with curry dishes. While they are simple, there is a trick to getting them to "puff" authentically. Lots of water in the dough, long kneading and resting allow the gluten to develop and hold the steam during cooking. Careful shaping to insure a smooth surface keeps the steam from escaping. Correct temperature and pressure allow the pockets of steam to develop. Even if the pockets don't develop, these are tasty flat breads. Indians use chapatis the same way Latin Americans use tortillas and Africans use injera.

Yield: 10 chapatis

2 cups whole wheat flour	**$\frac{1}{8}$ tsp salt**
1 tsp. oil	**$\frac{1}{2}$ cup (or more) lukewarm water**

1. Combine whole wheat flour, oil, and salt.
2. Gradually add some of the water.
3. Knead in additional water until the dough is soft and moist but not sticky. Knead 10-20 minutes.
4. At this point, the dough should set for 1-12 hours at room temperature. This resting time makes the dough easier to roll. However, it can be used immediately. Be sure to keep it moist.
5. When ready to use, divide the dough into 10 balls, rounding to make a smooth surface. Keep them covered with a damp cloth to avoid drying out.
6. Roll the balls into a 4"-6" circle, approximately $\frac{1}{4}$" thick.
7. Heat griddle to medium hot. (If it is too hot, the chapatis will burn; if not hot enough, they won't puff.)
8. Bake one chapati at a time. Turn to bake both sides.
9. After turning, use a hot pad or a spatula to apply pressure to the inside edges of the chapati to help it puff. Be careful not to burn yourself.
10. Chapatis are soft and pliable when warm. If you make them before you plan to serve them, reheat by wrapping stacks of chapatis in foil and warming in a 325° oven for 10-15 minutes. Sprinkle with water before reheating if the chapatis seem dry.

NATIVE AMERICAN FRY BREAD

I was introduced to fry bread at a festive Native American Day along the Natchez Trace in Mississippi. In a large iron kettle over an open fire, Choctaw Indians fried round flattened bits of dough. The fry breads disappeared as fast as they were made. I didn't get one that day, but I had observed the process. I went home and tried my own. You can, too. They're easy and fun to make.

Yield: 12-16 fry breads

¾ **cup whole wheat flour**　　**2 tsp. baking powder**
1½ **cups flour**　　　　　　　¾ **cup water**
¼ **tsp. salt**　　　　　　　　¼ **cup milk**

1. Sift flours, salt, and baking powder into a bowl.
2. Stir in water and milk.
3. Knead with hands.
4. Divide into 12 to 16 balls. Let rest covered for 10 minutes.
5. Roll or pat each ball into a circle approximately 5" in diameter. With fingers, make small hole in center.
6. Fry in several inches of hot oil at 390° for about 1 minute on each side, or until puffed and golden. Drain on absorbent paper.
7. Serve hot with honey.

Variation:
Replace whole wheat flour with 1 cup cornmeal, and decrease flour to 1 cup.

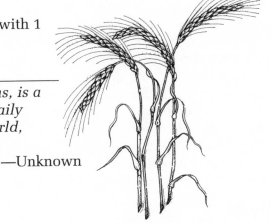

"Bread, in its many forms, is a welcome addition to our daily meals. For many in the world, bread is the only meal."
—Unknown

PITA BREAD

> Pocket Bread, Arab Bread, Syrian Bread!
> Make your own pocket bread. It's not difficult, and they taste terrific. Mixing, rolling, and shaping are easy. The secret to making good pocket bread is getting the baking right. Follow the procedure below very closely.

Yield: 6 pitas

1 cup warm water
1 pkg. dry yeast
1 tsp. brown sugar

1 cup whole wheat flour
2½ cups flour
½ tsp. salt

1. Dissolve yeast and brown sugar in warm water. Let set for 5 minutes.
2. Combine flours and salt in bowl and make a well in the center. Pour the yeast and water mixture into the well in the flour. Stir from center outward. Add more warm water or flour if necessary to make a very stiff dough.
3. Knead on a lightly floured board until smooth and elastic, about 10 minutes. Place in a greased bowl, turning once. Cover and let rise until double, about 30 to 45 minutes.
4. Punch down and return to floured board. Divide dough into 6 equal portions. Form each portion into a smooth ball. Place on a floured surface and cover with plastic wrap or a damp cloth. (Protecting the dough from drafts is essential to keep the surface from drying out.) Let rest for 10 to 15 minutes.
5. Preheat oven to 475°. Heat the cookie sheets by placing them upside down on bottom shelf of oven. (It is important to place dough on heated sheets.)
6. Carefully roll 3 balls of dough into 6" circles about ⅛" thick. Take care not to stretch, puncture, or crease dough. Work with enough flour so dough does not stick.
7. Place 3 rounds on hot cookie sheet. Bake for 5 to 6 minutes until puffed and set.

8. Remove from cookie sheet with hot pad or turner, leaving sheet in oven to stay hot while rolling next batch of 3. Bake one batch before rolling the next.

9. Place bread rounds on terry-cloth towel. Stack the pitas on top of each other as they come from the oven. Cover with another cloth while cooling (covering keeps pita soft). Keep covered until cool. When cool, store in plastic bags in refrigerator up to 1 month.

10. To serve, warm briefly in microwave or conventional oven. Cut pita bread in half crosswise. If pockets are not formed, slit with a knife.

Variation:
100% Whole Wheat Pita

3 cups whole wheat flour   **1 pkg. dry yeast**
1 cup water   **½ tsp. salt**

Follow directions on previous page.

"The bread which you do not use is the bread of the hungry; the garment hanging in your wardrobe is the garment of the one who is naked; the shoes you do not wear are the shoes of the one who is barefoot; the money that you keep locked away is the money of the poor; the acts of charity that you do not perform are so many injustices that you commit."
—St. Basil the Great

IRISH SODA BREAD

So easy to make; no yeast necessary.
Can be sliced like a yeast bread for sandwiches and toast or served hot.

Yield: 1 loaf

1½ cups whole wheat flour
½ cup flour
½ tsp. salt
1 tsp. baking soda
⅛ tsp. ground cardamom
(optional)

1 egg
1 Tbsp. honey
1 cup yogurt or buttermilk

1. Stir together flours, salt, baking soda, and cardamom.
2. Beat the egg. Add the honey and yogurt to the egg and beat.
3. Gradually pour egg mixture into the dry ingredients. Blend with a wooden spoon, or with your hands, to work in all of the flour. If too dry, add more yogurt. If too wet, add more flour.
4. Knead the bread for about 5 minutes, then shape into a flat but round loaf (see page 110).
5. Place loaf in a greased pie pan or on a baking sheet. Cut two parallel slashes in the dough about ½" deep, or sprinkle some additional flour on top of the loaf and make a cross in slashes with a sharp knife.
6. Bake at 375° for 25-35 minutes.

Variation:
Use all whole wheat flour.

"He who shares my bread and salt is not my enemy."
—Bedouin proverb

PAN DE AGUA

In the early '70s we lived in Puerto Rico. Once a day a man from the local bakery came through our neighborhood pushing a wooden cart stacked with long, fresh, crusty loaves of pan de agua, bread of water. As he pushed his wares through the street, he called, "Pan, Pan de agua." For just 25 cents, we could enjoy one of those loaves still warm from the oven.

Yield: 2 long loaves

¼ cup warm water
1 tsp. sugar
1 pkg. dry yeast
1 Tbsp. shortening
¾ tsp. salt

1 Tbsp. sugar
1 cup *hot* water
¾ cup whole wheat flour
2½-3 cups flour

1. Add 1 tsp. sugar to warm water.
2. Sprinkle yeast over water and let rest for 10 minutes.
3. In separate bowl, mix shortening, salt, sugar, and *hot* water.
4. When cooled to lukewarm, mix with yeast mixture.
5. Add whole wheat flour and flour gradually to form a mass that leaves the side of the bowl.
6. On lightly floured surface knead for 5 minutes. Place dough in greased bowl and let rise in warm place till double in size.
7. Form into 2 long loaves (see page 109). Place on greased baking sheet.
8. Let rise till double in size.
9. Bake at 400° for 25-30 minutes.

"A significant part of the pleasure of eating is in one's accurate consciousness of the lives and the world from which food comes."

—Wendell Berry

CHALLAH

This egg-rich, finely textured bread is an important part of a Jewish Sabbath meal. It is usually served as two braids, one on top of the other, symbolizing the double portion of manna their ancestors received on the sixth day of each week while wandering for 40 years. Manna was the "bread from heaven."

Yield: 2 loaves

1 cup very warm water	**¼ cup instant nonfat dry milk**
⅛ tsp. saffron	**1 tsp. salt**
1 pkg. dry yeast	**2 cups whole wheat flour**
¼ cup honey	**2½-3½ cups flour**
¼ cup oil	**1 tsp. cold water**
3 eggs	**poppy seeds**

1. Dissolve saffron in very warm water. When saffron is dissolved and water is warm, sprinkle yeast on saffron water and stir to dissolve. Let set 5 minutes.
2. Add honey, oil, 2 eggs, 1 egg white, dry milk, salt, and whole wheat flour to yeast mixture. Beat well.
3. Stir in enough flour to make a soft dough. Turn out onto lightly floured board. Knead until smooth and elastic, 8-10 minutes.
4. Place in greased bowl, turning to grease top. Cover. Let rise in warm place until doubled, about 1 hour.
5. Punch down. Divide dough in half.
6. Take half the dough and divide it into 2 pieces (one about one-third of dough and the other about two-thirds of dough): **Large piece:** Divide into 3 equal pieces. Roll each piece into a 12" rope. Braid the ropes together. Pinch ends to seal. **Small piece:** Divide into 3 equal pieces. Roll each piece into a

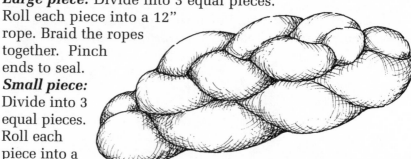

10" rope. Braid the ropes together. Place on top of large braid. Seal braids together at ends.

7. Place on greased baking sheet. Repeat with remaining dough to form second loaf.
8. Let rise in warm place until nearly doubled, 30-60 minutes.
9. Beat together remaining egg yolk and 1 tsp. cold water. Brush loaves with egg mixture. Sprinkle with poppy seeds.
10. Bake at 375° for 25-30 minutes, or until done. Cover with foil during the last 10 minutes to prevent over-browning, if necessary.

Blessed art Thou,
O Lord our God,
king of the world,
who bringest forth bread from the earth.
　　　　　　　　—Ancient Jewish Blessing

ITALIAN BREAD

Without lots of last minute preparation, you can have fresh hot Italian bread with your favorite Italian meal.

Yield: 2 long loaves or 6 large oval rolls

3½-4½ cups flour
1 Tbsp. sugar
1 Tbsp. salt
2 pkgs. dry yeast

1¾ cups very warm water
¾ cup whole wheat flour
1 Tbsp. oil

Glaze:
1 egg white   1 Tbsp. water

1. Combine 1½ cups flour, sugar, salt, and yeast.
2. Gradually add very warm water. Beat 2 minutes by hand.
3. Add whole wheat flour and oil. Beat vigorously by hand for 2 more minutes.
4. Stir in enough flour to make a stiff dough.
5. Turn out onto lightly floured board and knead until smooth and elastic, about 8-10 minutes.
6. Cover with plastic wrap; then a towel. Let rest 20 minutes.
7. **To Make Loaves:** Divide dough in half. Roll each half into an oblong, 15" x 10". Beginning at wide side, roll up tightly; pinch seam to seal. Taper ends by rolling gently back and forth.
   To Make Rolls: Divide dough into 6 equal pieces. Roll each piece into an oblong, 8" x 5". Beginning at wide side, roll up tightly; pinch seam to seal. Taper ends (see page 109).
8. Place on greased baking sheet sprinkled with cornmeal. Brush dough with oil. Cover loosely with plastic wrap. Refrigerate 2-24 hours.
9. When ready to bake, remove from refrigerator. Uncover dough carefully. Let stand at room temperature 10 minutes. Make 3-4 diagonal slashes on top of each loaf with a sharp knife.
10. Bake at 425° for 15 minutes for rolls, 20 minutes for loaves. Remove from oven and brush with egg white mixed with cold water. Return to oven; bake 5-10 minutes longer, or until golden brown.

WHOLE WHEAT BRIOCHES

Classic French topknots. No kneading is required, and the chilled dough is easy to shape.

Yield: 24 brioches

1 cup warm water	½ tsp. salt
1 pkg. dry yeast	3 eggs
1 tsp. sugar	¼ cup instant nonfat dry milk
⅓ cup oil	2 cups whole wheat flour
⅓ cup honey	2-2¼ cups flour

Glaze:

1 egg white	1 Tbsp. sugar

1. Dissolve yeast and l tsp. sugar in warm water. Let stand 5 minutes until yeast is bubbly.
2. In large bowl, mix the oil and honey. Add salt, eggs, dry milk, and whole wheat flour, mixing until smooth. Stir in yeast mixture. Beat well.
3. Beat in the flour to make a stiff dough. Cover dough with waxed paper and towel. Refrigerate overnight, or for at least 8 hours. Punch dough down once or twice as it rises.
4. Remove dough from refrigerator. Stir dough down. Place on lightly floured surface. Shape two-thirds of dough into 2" balls and place in greased muffin cups. Form equal number of small balls with remaining third of dough. Gently roll each of these balls into a cone shape. With a wet thumb, make an indentation in the center of each large ball. Place a small cone-shaped ball in each indentation. These cone-shaped pieces of dough form the "topknots."
5. Cover and let rise until double, about 40 minutes.
6. Beat egg white and 1 Tbsp. sugar slightly. Brush over rolls.
7. Bake at 375° for 15-20 minutes.

WHOLE WHEAT SCONES

Scones are a quick addition to any meal. The raisin or apple variations are especially good at breakfast; the cheese ones are delightful with soup for lunch.

Yield: 2 6" scones

1 cup whole wheat flour	**¹/₂ tsp. salt**
1 cup flour	**¹/₄ cup cold margarine *or* butter**
¹/₄ cup sugar	**1 egg**
2 tsp. baking powder	**²/₃ cup milk**

1. Combine flours, sugar, baking powder, and salt.
2. Cut in margarine until crumbly.
3. Mix egg and milk until frothy.
4. Combine wet and dry ingredients. Mix well to make a soft dough.
5. Turn out on lightly floured surface. Knead 8-10 times.
6. Divide into 2 equal portions.
7. Shape into 7" circles about ³/₄" thick. Place on a greased baking sheet. Cut the circles into 6 equal wedges, but do not separate. During baking the wedges will join together. However, they will break apart easily after baking.
8. Brush with milk and sprinkle with sugar, if desired.
9. Bake at 425° for 15 minutes. Scones can also be fried on a griddle in much the same way as English muffins. Place scones on medium hot griddle for 8-10 minutes; turn and bake other side.

Variations:
1. ***Yogurt:*** Replace the milk with ³/₄ cup yogurt and add ¹/₂ tsp. baking soda to the dry ingredients.

2. ***Cheese:*** Add 1 cup grated cheese to the dough. Sprinkle the shaped scones with sesame seeds before baking.

3. ***Raisin:*** Add ¹/₂ cup raisins to the dough.

4. ***Orange:*** Add 1 Tbsp. grated orange rind to the dough.

5. ***Apple:*** Add ¹/₂ cup grated apple to the dough and sprinkle the scones with cinnamon sugar.

POLENTA

Known as a "poor man's meal," this Italian dish is similar to cornmeal mush. However, the addition of cheese invites a tomato sauce topping more than the sweet toppings we suggest for mush.

Yield: Serves 6

5½ cups water

1 tsp. salt

2½ cups coarse cornmeal

1 cup cheese (optional)

1. Combine water and salt. Bring to a boil and slowly add cornmeal, taking a handful at a time and letting it run in a steady stream through your fingers while you stir the mixture continuously with a long wooden spoon.
2. The batter will begin to splatter as it thickens. Lower heat and continue to stir until your hand is tired and the polenta is really dense. It takes about 20 minutes.
3. At the end you can add a cup of cheese, cut into ½" pieces (not grated). Parmesan, Swiss, or cheddar cheese works well.
4. Pour the mixture onto a large platter. Shape into a rectangular loaf. Let set for 30-60 minutes before slicing. If desired, crisp the slices lightly under a broiler.
5. To serve, top it with a variety of Italian tomato-based sauces.

"Bread is all food; the rest is merely accompaniment."

—Italian proverb

MAIN DISHES

Well informed about health and nutrition, many Americans seem prepared to eat more whole grains. So how do we eat more complex carbohydrates, and how do we get 6-11 servings of grains a day? Perhaps the easiest way is to see grains as more than just bread.

Our image of grains has been limited to cereal for breakfast and a sandwich for lunch. We hope this collection of recipes will encourage you to broaden your vision and increase your repertoire of ways to serve grains. Here, for example, are ways to use whole grains in main dishes. The following chapter uses whole grains in desserts.

One of the simplest ways to add whole grains to one's diet is to include bread cubes in main dishes. See, for example, the recipes for Bread Stuffing, Bread Soufflé, Potato Filling Balls, and Oven Baked French Toast. This is also an excellent solution for leftover or stale bread. We've even found it to be a method for salvaging a loaf of fresh bread that didn't turn out right and didn't merit being served as sliced bread.

Some of our favorite main dishes start out with a yeast bread dough. When you make this dough with whole grains, you increase its nutritional value. So when you or your family crave a pizza, try Karen's Gourmet Pizza Dough for the crust—delicious health! Children love Bierrocks. Stuff them with Filling II and the Bierrocks become "Pizza Pockets." These are a favorite at the schools where I do consulting work.

We've all eaten noodles, but have you ever tried homemade whole wheat noodles or ravioli made with whole wheat? If you are trying to eat less meat, these noodles have so much flavor and texture that you won't miss the meat. In fact, we purposely choose some vegetarian toppings so we can better enjoy the whole wheat noodles.

Many cultures use whole grains in their main dishes. Scrapple is a traditional dish from our Pennsylvania Dutch heritage. Tennessee Corn Pone is a southern favorite. Some more ethnic breads that lend themselves to main dishes are the Injera, Chapati, and Tortilla recipes found in the Cultural Foods chapter.

If it's only making your own seasoned crumb mix with whole wheat bread crumbs or adapting your favorite waffle recipe to include whole wheat flour, start using whole grains in your main dishes, and reap the benefits of taste, nutrition, and health!

BREAD STUFFING

Mom always added melted butter to her stuffing. She would drizzle it over the bread cubes before mixing in the other ingredients. We loved to be around when she was doing this. We'd feast on bread cubes covered with melted butter!

Sometimes, for old times sake, I still drizzle a little melted butter over the bread cubes, but my dietitian conscience won't let me use much!

Yield: Serves 4

4 cups stale bread cubes (a mixture of cornbread and wheat bread is especially good)
½ cup minced celery
⅓ cup minced onion

½ tsp. salt
½ tsp. poultry seasoning
¼ tsp. pepper
1 egg
1½ cups milk

1. Combine bread, celery, onion, and seasonings.
2. Beat together egg and milk.
3. Add milk mixture to bread mixture. It should be quite moist. You may want to add more milk if the bread cubes are quite dry.
4. Pour into greased 1½ qt. casserole.
5. Bake covered at 350° for ½ hour.
6. Remove cover and continue baking 20-25 minutes.

HOMEMADE WHOLE WHEAT NOODLES

Homemade noodles are admittedly time-consuming, but delicious. So full of flavor, whole wheat noodles make other noodles seem flaccid. Whole wheat noodles are great served plain with a little butter and finely chopped parsley, as well as with many pasta dishes, soups, or vegetarian entrees.

Yield: 24 2" x 6" strips for lasagna, or,
12 4" x 6" rectangles for canneloni, or
96 ¹/₂" x 6" noodles or
20 ravioli

2 eggs	**¹/₂ tsp. salt**
¹/₄ cup water	**1³/₄ cups whole wheat flour**

1. Combine eggs, water, and salt, but just barely. The "stringiness" of the egg helps hold the dough together.
2. Measure whole wheat flour into a bowl and make a well in the center.
3. Drop the egg mixture into the well and work together with a fork or your fingers until ingredients are well mixed. Incorporate as much flour as necessary until the dough can be rolled in a ball and comes clean from your hands.
4. Knead the dough as you would for bread for 5-10 minutes. If dough seems dry, moisten your hands with water or oil and continue to knead until it is smooth and doesn't stick to your hands or the work surface.
5. Cover and set aside for 10-60 minutes.
6. Divide dough in half for ease in handling. Roll dough into long, paper-thin (¹/₁₆" thick) rectangles with a rolling pin. Keep turning the dough around and over as you roll. Cut into lengths or shapes desired. For ease in cutting thin noodles, roll dough into a neat tight jelly roll. Take a sharp knife and cut thin slices ¹/₄" or ¹/₂" wide. Unroll the noodles and let dry.
7. If planning to use immediately, let them dry for about 30 minutes. Cook in a large pot of rapidly boiling water for 5 to 8 minutes, depending on size of noodles. If not planning to use

immediately, allow noodles to dry completely by hanging them on wooden drying racks or over cloths on the backs of kitchen chairs. Store in a tight container in refrigerator until ready to use. Use within 3-4 days.

Variations:

1. If desired, you may add a dash or two of herbs to the noodle dough.

2. If you prefer lighter noodles, use 1 cup whole wheat flour and ¾ cup flour.

3. To make homemade ravioli with this dough, divide dough in half. Roll each half very thin.

    Spoon 1-2 tsp. of your favorite mixture (spinach, cheese, or meat) on one sheet of dough at regular intervals. Cover with second sheet of dough. Gently press down the spaces between the lumps of filling, and cut into squares with a knife or pizza crimper. If using a knife, be sure to seal edges by pressing down with a fork.

    Place ravioli in large pan of 3 qts. boiling water for 5-7 minutes. Serve with a pasta sauce and sprinkle with Parmesan cheese.

BIERROCKS

Bierrocks are pocket sandwiches with the filling baked right in the dough. Children enjoy helping to make these sandwiches—cutting out the dough and pinching the edges closed.

Yield: Serves 10

2 cups warm water	**1 egg**
2 pkgs. dry yeast	**¼ cup oil**
¼ cup sugar	**2 cups whole wheat flour**
1½ tsp. salt	**4-4½ cups flour**

1. Dissolve yeast in warm water.
2. Add sugar, salt, egg, oil, and whole wheat flour. Mix well.
3. Add enough additional flour to make a stiff dough.
4. Knead until smooth and elastic, approximately 10 minutes.
5. Place in a greased bowl, turning to grease top. Cover tightly. Dough may be allowed to rise at this point or refrigerated for several hours.
6. Meanwhile, prepare filling of choice. (See options beginning below.)
7. Punch down and roll the dough into thin sheets.
8. Cut into circles, squares, or rectangles, depending on the shape you want the bierrocks to be.
9. Place approximately ¼ cup of filling on each piece. Fold over and pinch edges of dough securely to seal.
10. Place on greased baking sheet. Let rise 15 minutes.
11. Bake at 375° for 20-30 minutes.

Filling 1

1½ lb. ground meat, turkey, beef, venison, or pork	**3 cups grated cabbage**
½ cup chopped onion	**½ tsp. pepper**
1½ tsp. salt	**dash hot pepper sauce, *or* chili powder**

1. Brown meat and onion in skillet.
2. Add other ingredients. Cover and cook over low heat, stirring occasionally, until cabbage is tender. Cool slightly.

Note:
Bierrocks with this filling are especially good served with a mustard sauce.

Filling 2

1½ lb. ground meat	1 cup of your favorite
½ cup chopped onion	tomato/pizza sauce *
	1 cup grated cheese

1. Brown meat and onion in skillet.
2. Add tomato sauce. Cook briefly. Cool slightly.
3. When making the bierrocks, place ¼ cup filling on dough and top with grated cheese.

* For Tomato Sauce, combine the following:

¾ cup tomato paste	1 tsp. oregano
¼ cup water	1 tsp. salt
2 tsp. sugar	⅛ tsp. pepper

Filling 3

3 cups vegetables of choice   1 cup grated cheese

1. Chop and cook vegetables until crisp tender. Asparagus, squash and onion, or mixed greens and spring onions are especially tasty.
2. Place ¼ cup vegetables on dough and top with grated cheese.

POT PIE

This recipe is from our great-grandmother, but my memories connected with this recipe include our grandfather, also. Grandma mixed the dough, but Grandpa always rolled it out, "thinner than any one else," he said. He believed the secret of good pot pie was in rolling the dough thin. Whenever I eat pot pie I can see Grandpa and Grandma working together in the kitchen. Today I have the solid wooden rolling pin that Grandpa used.

Yield: 60-70 2" squares of pot pie

1 cup flour	**¾ tsp. salt**
1 cup whole wheat flour	**1 egg**
2 tsp. baking powder	**6-7 Tbsp. milk**
1 Tbsp. shortening	

1. Mix flours, baking powder, shortening, and salt until crumbly.
2. To the flour mixture, add egg and enough milk to make a soft dough.
3. Roll out the dough as thin as possible. Cut into 2" squares with a knife or pastry wheel. Drop into boiling broth and cook about 20 minutes.
4. Sprinkle with fresh parsley and serve.

Note:

Pot Pie is a stew, usually chicken stew, that is cooked on top of the stove. To make: cook one 3 lb. stewing chicken in 2 quarts water until almost tender. Add 3-4 potatoes, peeled and cubed, 1 onion diced, and 1 carrot grated. Continue cooking until vegetables and meat are tender. Remove meat from bones and set aside. Bring broth to boil and drop pot pie squares into broth. Cook until tender. Add chicken meat to broth and serve hot. Sprinkle with fresh parsley.

PIZZA DOUGH

Yield: 1 14" pizza or 2 9" pan pizzas

1 pkg. dry yeast	2 Tbsp. olive or vegetable oil
1 tsp. sugar	1 cup whole wheat flour
1 cup warm water	2-2½ cups flour
¾ tsp. salt	

1. Combine yeast and sugar in water. Stir until dissolved.
2. Add salt, oil, whole wheat flour, and 1½ cups flour. Stir well.
3. Add enough remaining flour to make a soft dough.
4. Knead on lightly floured surface until smooth and elastic, about 5 minutes.
5. Place in greased bowl, turning to grease top.
6. Cover. Let rise in warm place until doubled, about 20-30 minutes.
7. Lightly grease 1 (14" round) or 2 (9" deep dish) pizza pan(s). Pat and stretch to fill pizza pan(s). Top pizza as desired.
8. Bake at 400° for 20 to 30 minutes or until done. Baking time depends on size, thickness of crust, and selected toppings.

Variations:

Cornmeal pizza dough: Omit whole wheat flour and use ½ cup cornmeal and 2½-3 cups flour.

Herbal pizza dough: Add 1½ tsp. dried basil, oregano, or rosemary leaves, and 1 clove finely minced garlic along with dry ingredients.

Pizza Make-Ahead Tip

Prepare pizza dough; let it rise once. Punch down and divide dough in half. Flatten each half to a 6" disk. Wrap, label, date, and freeze. The dough will keep up to 1 month in the freezer.

Thaw in refrigerator (8-16 hours), on counter top (2-4 hours), or in microwave oven (10 minutes on LOW. Turn dough over and rotate a quarter turn. Let rest 10 minutes. Repeat 1 or 2 times, until dough is thawed.) Check dough frequently as thawing time will vary according to size and the temperature of the dough, room, or refrigerator.

When thawed, proceed with Steps #7 and #8 above.

KAREN'S GOURMET PIZZA DOUGH

This recipe was created by Karen, our oldest daughter who is a graduate student in New York City. When she comes home and makes this for us, more than the crust is gourmet. She tops this crust with specialty mushrooms, peppers, black olives, sun-dried tomatoes, feta cheese, and fresh spinach.

This pizza dough is also versatile. It can be made, partially baked, and refrigerated for up to 6 days. Or it can be topped and baked immediately. This is handy if you have teenagers.

Yield: 2 14" round pizzas

2 cups warm water	1 tsp. salt
2 tsp. sugar	1 cup cornmeal
2 pkgs. dry yeast	4 cups whole wheat flour
1 Tbsp. olive oil	$\frac{1}{2}$ cup flour (for kneading)

1. Combine warm water and sugar. Sprinkle yeast over sugar water. Stir to dissolve. Let set 5 minutes.
2. Stir in oil, salt, cornmeal, and whole wheat flour.
3. Turn dough onto lightly floured surface and knead until smooth and elastic (about 5 minutes), using only as much additional flour as needed.
4. Place in greased bowl, turning to grease top. Cover and let rise in warm place until double in bulk, about 45 minutes.
5. Punch down and divide in half. Stretch each half into a 14" round on an ungreased baking sheet. Press around edge to form a standing rim of dough.
6. Bake at 350° for 10 minutes.
7. When cool, wrap tightly and store in refrigerator up to 6 days.
8. To serve, unwrap and place on ungreased baking sheet. Top with desired toppings. Bake at 425° for 20 minutes.

Variations:

1. Pizza dough can be shaped into individual pizzas.

2. If you wish to use pizza dough immediately, add toppings after Step 5, and bake at 400° for 25-30 minutes.

TENNESSEE CORN PONE

A wintertime favorite served with broccoli and cheese. I prefer a very juicy and spicy bean mixture, but you can vary that as you wish.

Yield: Serves 5-6

2 cups very juicy cooked
and seasoned beans
(a combination of cooked
beans including kidney,
pinto, and black beans is
delicious. Or use a thin
leftover bean chili.)

1 cup cornmeal
1 tsp. baking soda
½ tsp. salt
2 cups buttermilk
1 egg
2 Tbsp. margarine, melted

1. Heat beans until quite hot. Pour into a lightly greased 8" square baking dish.
2. In a medium bowl, mix the cornmeal, baking soda, and salt.
3. Combine with buttermilk, egg, and melted margarine.
4. Stir the wet and dry ingredients together until smooth and pour them over the hot beans.
5. Bake at 425° on top rack of oven for about 30 minutes, or until cornbread becomes a rich golden color and pulls away from the sides of the pan.

WHOLE WHEAT DUMPLINGS

Dumplings are starchy, savory bits of dough, cooked in hot stock.

Yield: 15-20 dumplings

¾ **cup whole wheat flour**   1 **egg**
¾ **cup flour**   3-4 **Tbsp. milk**
3 **tsp. baking powder**   2-3 **qts. broth or stew**
½ **tsp. salt**

1. Stir flours, baking powder, and salt together.
2. Combine egg and milk. Stir into dry ingredients to make a biscuit-like dough.
3. Drop by small spoonfuls into 2-3 quarts boiling broth or stew. Cover tightly. Cook on low heat 12-15 minutes.

CORNMEAL DUMPLINGS
Yield: Approximately 15 dumplings

¾ cup water
½ cup cornmeal
1 egg
¼ tsp. salt
¼ tsp. paprika

1½ tsp. minced onion
1 tsp. finely chopped fresh herbs
(sage and basil) or ¼-½ tsp.
dried herbs, crumbled
3 quarts vegetable stock

1. Boil water. Gradually whisk in cornmeal. Stir slowly and then beat vigorously. Turn heat down to very low. Cook, stirring constantly with wooden spoon, about 3 minutes.
2. Remove from heat. Beat the batter to cool it slightly.
3. Beat in egg. Stir in seasonings, onion, and herbs.
4. Let batter cool until lukewarm.
5. Drop by small spoonfuls into 3 quarts boiling stock. Cover tightly. Cook on low heat 15 minutes.

Tips for Perfect Dumplings

- Use enough liquid to cook dumplings, at least 3 quarts.

- Use large pot with wide surface and high sides.

- Don't crowd the dumplings. They need room to expand with hot liquid on all sides.

- Don't make dumplings too large or the insides will be underdone.

- Roll dumplings in flour or meal to help hold them together.

- Stock must be boiling when dumplings are dropped in, but not boiling hard.

- Dumplings are cooked by steam. Put cover on pot once you've put the dumplings in, and don't lift the lid until the time specified by the recipe has elapsed.

SCRAPPLE

Grandpa and Grandma's visits were always exciting, but especially in the fall. Fall was butchering time! For years Grandpa and Grandma went to market in Lancaster County, Pennsylvania, selling their baked goods and farm products. What I know of butchering I owe to them.

Usually the men did the slaughtering, but once the meat was ready to be "worked up," the women and children came. We cut the meat into portions, trimmed the fat for lard, and put all the bones and scraps of meat into a big iron kettle. These scraps and bones cooked all day in water while we butchered. After this was well cooked, we strained the broth, picked the meat from the bones, and ground it. This broth and meat were used to make scrapple.

This is our grandparents' recipe:

1 bucket meat	1½ oz. pepper
2 buckets broth and water	6 lbs. cornmeal
½ lb. salt	2 lbs. whole wheat flour

While I don't have buckets of meat and broth now, I still enjoy scrapple and make it from venison, chicken, pork, beef, or some combination of meat using the following adaptation.

1 qt. broth or water	1½ cups cornmeal
2 cups cooked ground meat	½ cup whole wheat flour
1½ tsp. salt	1 cup cold water
¼ tsp. pepper	

1. In a heavy bottom saucepan, cook together broth, meat, and spices.
2. Mix cornmeal and flour with 1 cup cold water.
3. Remove broth from heat and gradually add flour mixture to it. Return to heat and stir constantly until thickened.
4. Reduce heat, cover, and cook 20 minutes. Stir occasionally.
5. Remove from heat and pour into greased loaf pans. Chill.
6. Cover and refrigerate or freeze.

7. When ready to use, slice ¹/₂" thick. Dust with flour. Fry on lightly greased griddle until crisp. You can omit the dusting with flour, place scrapple on lightly greased baking sheets, and broil until brown and crisp.

8. Serve with apple butter or syrup, or ketchup, mustard, and horseradish.

Variations:

1. To increase the nutritional value, add grated carrots, onion, or celery to the broth.

2. Additional spices can be added: try ¹/₂ tsp. poultry seasoning or ¹/₄ tsp. savory or sage.

3. "Panhas" (which I learned from my husband's family) is similar, but made with just the broth (no meat) and cornmeal (no whole wheat flour).

WAFFLES

As children, we loved waffles with turkey gravy for Sunday dinner. We also liked to put butter and sugar on the waffles. The rule at our home was: after eating one waffle with gravy, we could eat one with butter and sugar. On the other hand, my husband grew up enjoying his waffles with cheese and maple syrup. But we all agree, the fun was in filling the holes.

Today, along with the traditional ways of filling the holes, we have added yogurt spreads. We also enjoy waffles and ice cream for dessert. We dip "leftover" waffles, which we always make sure to have, in beaten egg and fry them like French toast for breakfast.

Yield: 4-14 waffles, depending on the size of the waffle iron

4 eggs, separated
2½ cups milk
½ cup melted margarine
2 cups whole wheat flour

2 cups flour
2 Tbsp. baking powder
1 tsp. salt
2 Tbsp. sugar (optional)

1. Separate eggs. Beat egg whites till soft peaks form. Set aside.
2. Beat egg yolks well. Combine yolks, milk, and margarine.
3. Combine the flours, baking powder, salt, and sugar (if desired).
4. Add dry ingredients to milk mixture. Stir just until combined.
5. Fold in egg whites. Do not over-mix.
6. Bake according to waffle iron directions.
7. Serve with syrup, cheese and syrup, peanut butter/yogurt, applesauce/yogurt, gravy, etc.

Variations:
For Buttermilk Waffles: Substitute 3 cups buttermilk for 2½ cups milk in the above recipe and add ¾ tsp. baking soda.

For Pecan Waffles: After pouring batter onto waffle iron, sprinkle with a few pecans and bake.

For Carob or Cocoa Waffles: Add ⅓ cup carob *or* cocoa powder to dry ingredients.

CORNMEAL QUICHE

Yield: Serves 6

Crust

½ cup cornmeal
¾ cup flour
½ tsp. salt

⅛ tsp. pepper
⅓ cup soft shortening
3 Tbsp. cold water

1. Combine cornmeal, flour, salt, and pepper.
2. Cut in shortening.
3. Sprinkle cold water over dry mixture while tossing with a fork. Stir lightly until mixture forms a ball. Roll out on lightly floured board or between two sheets of waxed paper.
4. Fit loosely into 9" pie pan. Finish edge as desired.

Filling

1¼ cups grated cheese
1¾ cups whole kernel corn, fresh or frozen
1 Tbsp. minced onion
4 large eggs

1 cup evaporated milk
1 tsp. salt
¼ tsp. cayenne
1 Tbsp. parsley

5. Sprinkle 1 cup cheese on bottom of unbaked crust.
6. Spread corn and onion over cheese.
7. Combine eggs, milk, salt, and cayenne. Beat until well blended.
8. Pour over corn. Sprinkle with remaining ¼ cup cheese and parsley.
9. Place on bottom rack of oven. Bake at 425° for 15 minutes. Reduce temperature to 350° and continue baking 25-30 minutes. Remove from oven and let stand 5-10 minutes before cutting and serving.

Note:
The evaporated milk in the above recipe can be replaced with ½ cup instant nonfat dry milk and ¾ cup water.

POTATO-FILLING BALLS

Moist and delicious! Serve with the Christmas turkey and start a family tradition.

Yield: 10-12 servings

10-12 cups soft bread cubes
½ cup minced onion
1-1½ cups minced celery
2 Tbsp. chopped parsley
½ cup melted butter

1½ cups milk or enough
to moisten cubes
2 beaten eggs
1½ cups mashed potatoes
salt and pepper to taste

1. Place bread cubes in large mixing bowl.
2. Add onion, celery, parsley, butter, milk, eggs, mashed potatoes, and seasonings. Mix well.
3. Use an ice cream scoop to shape into balls. Place on buttered baking sheet. Drizzle with additional melted butter, if desired.
4. Bake uncovered at 375° for 20 minutes.

Note:
Filling can also be spread in a greased 9" x 13" baking pan and baked for 30-35 minutes.

If desired, sauté onions and celery in butter before combining with the other ingredients.

"Don't throw away leftover food. Keep serving it and you will be satisfied."

—A Ugandan proverb

BREAD SOUFFLÉ

This delightful vegetarian entreé is a good way to use stale breads and cheeses which are aging. Try rye bread cubes with Swiss cheese or whole wheat bread cubes with cheddar cheese.

Yield: Serves 4

2½ cups milk
1 qt. bread cubes
4 eggs
¾ tsp. salt

¼ tsp. pepper
¼ tsp. dry mustard
2 cups grated cheese

1. Warm milk and pour over bread cubes.
2. Beat eggs and dry seasonings well.
3. Combine the bread, eggs, and cheese.
4. Pour into a greased 2-quart casserole or a 9" square pan.
5. Bake at 350° for 30-40 minutes, or until set.

Variations:

1. Add ½ to 1 cup sautéed or cooked vegetables before baking. Try one or more of the following: onions, green peppers, mushrooms, broccoli, asparagus.

2. For a French toast casserole: Use 1½ qt. bread cubes, do not heat the milk, omit the dry mustard and cheese. Add 1 Tbsp. sugar and ½ tsp. vanilla to the milk. Bake as directed and serve with maple syrup, honey, or fruit and yogurt.

CREPES

Yield: Serves 2

¾ cup whole wheat flour   ½ Tbsp. oil
1 cup milk   ¼ tsp. salt
1 egg

1. Blend all ingredients together in blender at low speed. Batter can be refrigerated for 1 hour or more at this point.
2. Pour ¼ cup or less batter onto a hot, lightly oiled, or non-stick, fry pan. Immediately tilt pan to spread batter over the pan.
3. Fry briefly (approximately 30 seconds) until slightly brown. Turn and fry briefly on other side.
4. Remove from pan. Stack on a plate and cover with damp cloth.
5. Fill with desired filling. (See Filling options below.)
6. Bake at 400° for 15-20 minutes.
7. Serve hot with a sauce if desired. (See Sauce options below.)

Cheese Filling

1 cup cottage cheese   2 Tbsp. chopped nuts
1 Tbsp. sugar

Mix together and put 1-2 Tbsp. on each crepe. Fold in opposite sides and then roll up. Place seam side down in a greased baking dish.

Vegetable Filling

2 cups diced asparagus   ¼ cup finely chopped onion

Cook together until crispy tender. Put 1-2 Tbsp. on each crepe. Turn in opposite sides and then roll up. Place seam side down in a greased baking dish.

Sauces

Serve cheese-filled crepes with Yogurt and Applesauce (see page 132).

Serve vegetable-filled crepes with a cheese sauce.

SEASONED CRUMB MIX

Use to coat chicken or fish.

Yield: About 2 cups

1³/₄ cups dry bread crumbs
1 tsp. salt
1 tsp. paprika
1 tsp. celery salt
¹/₂ tsp. onion salt
¹/₈ tsp. pepper

1 Tbsp. parsley
2 Tbsp. oil (optional)
¹/₄ cup Parmesan cheese
   (optional)
¹/₂ tsp. poultry seasoning
   (optional)

1. Blend ingredients until well mixed.
2. When ready to use, put ¹/₂ cup crumb mix in a paper or plastic bag. Moisten fish or chicken with milk and shake one piece at a time in bag. Add more mix as needed.
3. Place chicken or fish in lightly oiled pan. Bake chicken for 1 hour and fish for 30 minutes at 350°.
4. Crumb mix keeps unrefrigerated in tightly covered container.

*Be gentle
  when you touch bread.
    Let it not lie
      uncared for, unwanted.
        So often bread
          is taken for granted.*

*There is so much beauty
  in bread—
Beauty of sun and soil,
Beauty of patient toil.
Winds and rains have caressed it,
    Christ often blessed it.
Be gentle
  when you touch bread.*
                    —Author unknown

OVEN BAKED FRENCH TOAST

This makes a delightful breakfast or brunch dish. It is like eating sticky buns without having to go through the lengthy process of making them, or having French toast with the syrup cooked in it.

Yield: 4 servings

8 slices French bread, 1" thick	**⅛ tsp. nutmeg**
4 eggs	**½ tsp. cinnamon**
2 cups skim milk	**½ cup brown sugar packed**
1 tsp. vanilla	**1 Tbsp. dark corn syrup**
	¾ cup coarsely chopped pecans

1. Place single layer of bread slices in buttered baking pan.
2. Combine eggs, milk, vanilla, nutmeg, and cinnamon. Pour over bread slices. Cover and refrigerate overnight.
3. Combine brown sugar, corn syrup, and pecans. Sprinkle evenly over bread.
4. Bake at 350° for 25 minutes until puffy and golden.
5. Serve warm. Serving with additional syrup is an option, but not necessary.

DESSERTS

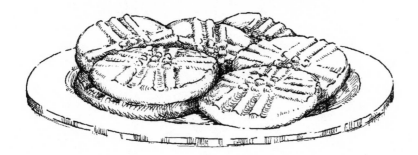

One of the principles we work with in our local Head Start Program is that food is not to be used as a reward. We implement the rule by serving all meals as a unit. No longer are children told as we were: "If you clean your plate, you may have dessert." Dessert, if any, is part of the meal and contributes to the overall nutritional quality of the child's diet.

Our hope is that these recipes will do just that. We don't recommend serving dessert at every meal, unless you consider a piece of fresh fruit a dessert. When you do choose to offer dessert, consider a recipe which includes whole grains.

Many of our favorites feature the winning combination of whole grains and fruit. Apples and whole wheat combine in Honey Apple Cake and Fresh Apple Cake. Blueberries and cornmeal create an unusual and pleasing combination in Blueberry Cornmeal Loaf Cake. Hard Cake with Strawberries is a natural. And cobblers, crumbles, turnovers, and dumplings all use fruits and whole grains.

Surprisingly, vegetables even find their way into some of these recipes. Carrots are the focus in Whole Wheat Carrot Cake and Shaggy Carrot Cookies. The infamous zucchini does famously in Zucchini Carob Cake. Even potatoes find their way into cakes: Carob Potato Cake.

Who would think that desserts could be made with leftovers? But bread puddings are an easy and delicious way to use up leftover bread. And Molasses Pie features bread crumbs.

Head Start rules aside, just in case you want to use food as a reward, or need an ultimate bargaining tool, try a Chewy Granola Bar or a slice of Whole Wheat Brownie Pie!

CHOCO-NUT BREAD PUDDING

Who would ever think that leftover stale bread could become so gourmet? This is a great dish to take to a group gathering. It is sure to get rave reviews.

Yield: 6-8 servings

4 cups whole wheat bread, cubed
¹/₃ cup flaked coconut
¹/₃ cup chocolate *or* carob chips
¹/₃ cup sugar

¹/₂ cup peanut butter, preferably crunchy
2 eggs
1 tsp. vanilla
dash of salt
2¹/₂ cups milk

1. Place bread cubes in an 8" square baking dish.
2. Sprinkle with coconut and chocolate pieces.
3. In small mixing bowl thoroughly blend sugar, peanut butter, eggs, vanilla, salt, and milk.
4. Pour over bread.
5. Place baking dish in a shallow pan on oven rack. Pour hot water into outer pan to depth of 1 inch.
6. Bake at 350° for 1 hour, or till a knife inserted halfway between the edge and the center comes out clean.
7. Serve warm or cold. Store in the refrigerator.

Variation:
Substitute ¹/₃ cup raisins for chocolate chips. Add ¹/₂ tsp. cinnamon.

BASIC BREAD PUDDING

A simple recipe with some delightful variations.

Yield: Serves 6

2 eggs	**¼ tsp. salt**
2⅓ cups milk	**½ tsp. vanilla**
⅓ cup sugar	**4 cups bread, cubed**

1. Beat eggs.
2. Add milk, sugar, salt, and vanilla. Mix well. Pour mixture over bread cubes and stir to moisten.
3. Pour into greased 1½ qt. baking dish or 8" or 9" square pan.
4. Bake at 350° for 45-55 minutes, or until knife inserted into middle of pudding comes out clean. Serve warm or cold.

Variations:
Strawberry Bread Pudding

1 10 oz. pkg. frozen strawberries, thawed
2 Tbsp. cornstarch

1. In saucepan, combine undrained strawberries and cornstarch.
2. Cook and stir over medium heat until mixture thickens and bubbles.
3. Spread evenly over bottom of 9" square pan. Carefully pour Bread Pudding mixture (given above) over berries.
4. Bake as directed in Step #4 above.

Applesauce Bread Pudding

⅔ cup applesauce	**2 Tbsp. brown sugar**
½ tsp. cinnamon	**⅓ cup raisins**

1. Combine applesauce, cinnamon, brown sugar, and raisins.
2. Follow above recipe through Step #3.
3. Pour applesauce mixture over Bread Pudding mixture.
4. Bake as directed in Step #4 above.

Cottage Cheese Bread Pudding

1 cup cottage cheese   **¹/₄ tsp. nutmeg**

Add cottage cheese and nutmeg to other ingredients in Step #2 of
the Basic Bread Pudding Recipe and continue with recipe.

NATIVE AMERICAN CORN PUDDING

An unusual "rice pudding-like" dessert with the taste of corn.

Yield: Serves 4-6

4 cups milk   **¹/₂ tsp. ginger**
¹/₃ cup cornmeal   **¹/₂ tsp. cinnamon**
¹/₃ cup molasses   **¹/₄ tsp. salt**

1. In saucepan, scald milk. Bubbles will appear around the edge
   of the pan. This is the boiling point. Do not boil.
2. Remove from heat. Sprinkle in cornmeal, stirring to combine.
3. Return to heat. Cook slowly, stirring often for 10 minutes.
4. Add molasses, ginger, cinnamon, and salt. Pour into a buttered
   baking dish.
5. Bake uncovered at 325° for 1 hour, stirring every
   15 minutes during the first half hour of baking.
6. Chill and serve drizzled with molasses or
   maple syrup.

HONEY APPLE CAKE

Using both apples and applesauce makes this cake doubly flavorful and moist.

Yield: 1 8" square single layer cake

¼ cup shortening
½ cup honey
1 egg
1 cup plus 2 Tbsp.
  whole wheat flour
2 Tbsp. instant nonfat
  dry milk
½ tsp. baking soda
½ tsp. baking powder

½ tsp. salt
¼ tsp. cinnamon
⅛ tsp. cloves
¼ cup applesauce
½ cup chopped apples
⅓ cup chopped nuts
⅓ cup raisins (optional)
confectioners' sugar

1. Beat shortening with honey on high speed of electric mixer till light and fluffy.
2. Beat in egg.
3. In another bowl stir together flour, dry milk, baking soda, baking powder, salt, cinnamon, and cloves. Add to creamed mixture alternately with applesauce.
4. Fold in apples, nuts, and raisins (optional).
5. Spread batter in a greased 8" square baking pan.
6. Bake at 350° for 20-25 minutes, or till cake tests done. Dust with confectioners' sugar before serving.

FRESH APPLE CAKE

Chunks of apples dot this cake. If you are using good, fresh, organic apples with soft skins, don't peel the apples. The skin adds important fiber and interesting color.

Yield: 9" x 13" cake

1 cup sugar	1 tsp. cinnamon
1 cup whole wheat flour	$\frac{1}{3}$ cup oil
1$\frac{1}{4}$ cups flour	2 eggs
$\frac{1}{4}$ tsp. salt	1 cup yogurt
$\frac{1}{2}$ tsp. baking powder	1$\frac{1}{2}$ tsp. vanilla
1$\frac{1}{2}$ tsp. baking soda	3 cups apples, chopped
$\frac{1}{2}$ tsp. cloves	

Topping:

$\frac{1}{3}$ cup brown sugar	1 Tbsp. melted margarine
2 tsp. flour	$\frac{1}{4}$ cup rolled oats
2 tsp. cinnamon	$\frac{1}{2}$ cup chopped nuts or coconut

1. Combine dry ingredients: sugar, flours, salt, baking powder, baking soda, cloves, and cinnamon.
2. Combine the oil, eggs, yogurt, and vanilla. Mix well.
3. Mix together the wet and dry ingredients.
4. Fold in the apples.
5. Pour into a greased 9" x 13" pan.
6. Combine topping ingredients and sprinkle over top of batter.
7. Bake at 350° for 35-40 minutes.

WHOLE WHEAT CARROT CAKE

Carrot cake is loved for its delicious flavor and cream cheese frosting, not necessarily its nutritional value. However, this carrot cake wins nutritional stars for its exclusive use of whole wheat flour, minimal amount of oil, the addition of buttermilk, and a yogurt cheese frosting. The result is more fiber and less fat, but the same moist, tender, rich flavor.

Yield: 9" x 13" cake

2 cups whole wheat flour	1 cup buttermilk *or* yogurt
2 tsp. baking powder	2 tsp. vanilla
1½ tsp. baking soda	1 cup well drained crushed
½ tsp. salt	pineapple
2 tsp. cinnamon	2 cups finely grated carrots
1 cup brown sugar	1 cup flake coconut
3 eggs	1 cup walnuts
¼ cup oil	

1. Sift together flour, baking powder, baking soda, salt, cinnamon, and brown sugar.
2. Beat eggs until lemon colored. Add oil, buttermilk, and vanilla. Stir in flour mixture.
3. Stir in pineapple, carrots, coconut, and nuts.
4. Pour batter into greased 9" x 13" pan. Bake at 350° for 50-60 minutes, or until cake tests done when wooden pick is inserted in center.
5. If desired, dust with confectioners' sugar or frost with yogurt cheese frosting.

Yogurt Cheese Frosting:

¼ cup yogurt cheese	2½ cups confectioners' sugar
½ tsp. vanilla	2 tsp. margarine

Combine above ingredients and spread on cooled cake. Refrigerate.

ZUCCHINI CAROB CAKE

When the zucchini plants are producing their notoriously bountiful harvest, the question around our house is not, "What is for dinner?" but rather, "How are you fixing the zucchini today?" A favorite dessert is this very moist and full flavored cake.

Yield: 9" x 13" cake

3 eggs
¹⁄₂ cup brown sugar
¹⁄₂ cup sugar
¹⁄₄ cup oil
¹⁄₂ cup applesauce
1 tsp. vanilla
¹⁄₂ cup buttermilk
1¹⁄₂ cups whole wheat flour
1 cup flour

¹⁄₂ tsp. allspice
¹⁄₂ tsp. cinnamon
¹⁄₂ tsp. salt
2 tsp. baking soda
¹⁄₄ cup carob *or* cocoa powder
2-3 cups grated zucchini
¹⁄₂-1 cup carob *or* chocolate chips
¹⁄₂ cup nuts (optional)

1. Beat eggs. Add sugars, oil, applesauce, vanilla, and buttermilk. Mix well.
2. Sift flours, allspice, cinnamon, salt, baking soda, and carob powder together. Stir zucchini into dry ingredients.
3. Add dry ingredients to the wet ingredients. Mix well.
4. Turn into a greased and floured 9" x 13" pan. Sprinkle chips and nuts (optional) on top.
5. Bake at 325° for 45 minutes.

Note:
1. This works well made into cupcakes.
2. With the chips and nuts sprinkled on top, icing isn't necessary. But sometimes we like to spread it with a Peanut Butter Frosting:

2 cups confectioners' sugar
¹⁄₄ cup peanut butter

¹⁄₂ tsp. vanilla
enough milk to make a spreading consistency

Beat together till smooth.

CAROB POTATO CAKE

Cake is moist and has a firm texture.

Yield: 9" x 13" cake

3 eggs	1 tsp. baking soda
1 cup sugar	1 tsp. baking powder
¼ cup oil	1 tsp. cinnamon
1 cup mashed potatoes	¼ tsp. nutmeg
¾ cup applesauce	¼ tsp. cloves
1 tsp. vanilla	½ tsp. salt
1½ cups whole wheat flour	1 cup yogurt
⅓ cup carob *or* cocoa powder	

1. Beat eggs. Add sugar and continue beating till thick and lemon colored.
2. Add oil and mashed potatoes. Beat till thoroughly blended.
3. Add applesauce and vanilla. Mix well.
4. Sift together whole wheat flour, carob, baking soda, baking powder, cinnamon, nutmeg, cloves, and salt.
5. Add sifted dry ingredients to creamed wet ingredients, alternating with yogurt. Beat till smooth.
6. Pour batter into a greased and floured 9" x 13" pan. (If desired, sprinkle batter with carob chips and chopped nuts, about ⅓ cup of each.)
7. Bake at 350° for 35-40 minutes, or until cake tests done.

BLUEBERRY CORNMEAL LOAF CAKE

My husband and I raise and sell blueberries, as well as grind and sell cornmeal. I've found this recipe creates lots of business and makes friends.

Yield: 1 loaf

1 cup fresh or frozen
  (not thawed) blueberries
1 Tbsp. flour
1½ cups flour
½ cup cornmeal
2 tsp. baking powder
⅔ cup sugar
½ tsp. salt

½ cup yogurt
¼ cup water
1 Tbsp. lemon juice
1 large egg
¼ cup oil
1 tsp. grated lemon rind
2 tsp. cinnamon sugar

1. Preheat oven to 350°.
2. Toss blueberries with 1 Tbsp. flour and set aside.
3. Sift together flour, cornmeal, baking powder, sugar, and salt.
4. In a small bowl mix together yogurt, water, lemon juice, egg, oil, and lemon rind.
5. Add liquids to dry ingredients and mix well.
6. Gently fold in blueberries.
7. Spoon batter into greased 8" x 4" loaf pan.
8. Sprinkle with cinnamon sugar.
9. Bake for 50 minutes, or until cake is golden and toothpick inserted into the center comes out clean. You may want to cover loosely with foil during the last half hour to prevent excess browning.

HARD CAKE

In our home, we always used this Hard Cake recipe from our grandmother for strawberry shortcake. A June supper favorite was warm Hard Cake, covered with freshly picked strawberries and rich cream. Ummm! We still love Hard Cake and fresh strawberries, but we've replaced the rich cream with cold skim milk!

1 cup flour	2½ tsp. baking powder
1 cup whole wheat flour	⅓ cup shortening
1 cup sugar	½ cup milk
1 tsp. salt	

1. Mix flour, whole wheat flour, sugar, salt, and baking powder. Cut in shortening to make fine crumbs.
2. Remove about ½ cup crumbs. Reserve for top of cake.
3. Add milk to remaining crumbs. Mix briefly.
4. Pat into a greased 9" pie pan.
5. Top with reserved crumbs.
6. Bake at 350° for 30 minutes.

Variation:
For a more biscuit-like shortcake, decrease the sugar to 2 Tbsp. and increase the milk to 1 cup. Do not remove ½ cup crumbs (as described above in Step #2). Otherwise, proceed according to instructions above.

OLD-FASHIONED GINGERBREAD

Yield: 1 8" square gingerbread

½ cup shortening
¼ cup brown sugar
1 egg
1 cup dark molasses
1½ cups flour
1 cup whole wheat flour
½ tsp. salt

½ tsp. baking soda
1 tsp. baking powder
1½ tsp. ginger
1 tsp. cinnamon
¼ tsp. allspice
1 cup boiling water

1. Cream shortening.
2. Add brown sugar gradually and beat until fluffy.
3. Add egg and beat well.
4. Blend molasses into mixture.
5. Sift flours, salt, baking soda, baking powder, and spices together. Add dry ingredients gradually to mixture.
6. Add boiling water and stir until batter is smooth. Batter will be thin.
7. Pour into greased and floured 8" square baking pan.
8. Bake at 350° for 40 to 45 minutes.
9. Serve warm topped with Yogurt and Applesauce (page 132) or Lemon Sauce (page 220).

Variation:
To reduce fat, substitute ¼ cup pumpkin and ¼ cup oil for the ½ cup shortening.

LEMON SAUCE

Yield: About 1 cup

⅓ **cup sugar**	**1 tsp. margarine**
1 Tbsp. cornstarch	**1½ Tbsp. lemon juice**
1 cup water	**grated rind from one lemon**
	(approx. 1 Tbsp.)

1. Mix sugar and cornstarch in saucepan.
2. Gradually add water.
3. Cook over medium heat, stirring constantly till mixture thickens and boils. Boil 1 minute.
4. Remove from heat. Stir in margarine, lemon juice, and lemon rind.
5. Serve warm over gingerbread.

WHOLE WHEAT PIE CRUST

Grandma always preferred lard for the shortening in pie crusts. Sometimes my dietitian's conscience bothers me and I use a vegetable shortening. At other times I say, since any pastry has a lot of fat and isn't good for anyone, why not just enjoy it? If you indulge, "sin boldly!"

Yield: Crusts for 5 9" pies

2 cups whole wheat flour	**1¼ cups shortening or lard**
2 cups flour	**½ cup water**
1 Tbsp. sugar	**1 large egg**
2 tsp. salt	**1 Tbsp. vinegar**

1. Mix together flours, sugar, and salt.
2. Cut in shortening until crumbly but not fine crumbs.
3. Briefly mix together water, egg, and vinegar. Do not beat.
4. Add liquids to flour and mix with a fork to moisten evenly. Form into a ball.
5. On lightly floured surface, divide dough into 5 equal pieces. For ease in rolling, flour surface of dough piece and roll between two sheets of waxed paper. Peel top sheet off, invert rolled pie dough over pie pan, and peel off bottom sheet of waxed paper which is now on the top.

    Do not stretch the dough when you tuck the lower edge of the pastry into the pan. If stretched, it will shrink when it bakes and the top edge will pull down, leaving a low spot where filling can run out.
6. Fill as desired and bake as directed.

Note: This is an easy crust to handle and can be re-rolled without toughening. It also keeps in the refrigerator for up to 2 weeks. It keeps very well for months frozen. To freeze, shape the divided pieces of dough into disks about 4" in diameter. Freeze individually wrapped and in an airtight plastic bag.

MOLASSES PIE

I recently described this pie as a combination of or cross between gingerbread and Pennsylvania Dutch shoofly pie. The ginger flavor is fairly pronounced, especially if you eat the pie warm. If you like, you can reduce the ginger to ½ teaspoon.

Yield: 1 8" round pie

3 Tbsp. margarine
¾ cup boiling water
1 tsp. baking soda
1 cup dark molasses
¾ cup dried whole wheat
  bread crumbs

¼ cup chopped nuts
¼ cup raisins
1 cup whole wheat flour
¾ tsp. salt
1 tsp. ginger
¼ cup wheat germ

1. Place margarine in mixing bowl.
2. Pour boiling water over margarine.
3. Combine baking soda and molasses. Add to water and margarine.
4. Add bread crumbs, nuts, and raisins.
5. Combine whole wheat flour, salt, ginger, and wheat germ. Add to above. Stir to combine.
6. Pour into greased 8" round layer cake pan.
7. Bake at 325° for 30-35 minutes.
8. Serve warm or cool. Delicious with a frosty mixture of equal parts applesauce and yogurt (see page 132).

Variation:
At Step 6, pour the batter into a 9" unbaked pie crust. Bake at 350° for 35-40 minutes. Serve as suggested in Step 8.

To Prevent Soggy Crusts
1. Brush unbaked crust lightly with unbeaten egg white and let it dry before pouring in the filling.
2. Sprinkle the unbaked crust lightly with a mixture of equal parts sugar and flour before adding filling.

WHOLE WHEAT BROWNIE PIE

I first used this recipe as the cake for my husband's 37th birthday several (?) years ago. It has become such a favorite that we find many excuses other than birthdays to make Brownie Pie.

Yield: 1 9" pie

⅓ **cup oil**
⅓ **cup sugar**
⅓ **cup honey**
2 tsp. vanilla
2 eggs

⅓ **cup whole wheat flour**
⅓ **cup toasted or raw wheat germ**
⅓ **cup carob or cocoa powder**
¼ **tsp. salt**

1. Beat oil, sugar, honey, and vanilla together.
2. Add eggs one at a time.
3. Stir together whole wheat flour, wheat germ, carob powder, and salt. Add to wet mixture, beating just until blended.
4. Pour into a greased 9" pie pan.
5. Bake at 350° for 25 minutes.

Variation:
Sprinkle with ¼ cup chopped nuts or sunflower seeds before baking.

". . . baking is more than mere mechanics, mixing this and that and putting it in the oven. . . home-baking is part of a continuum, a small link in the chain that unites us as human beings. When you bake, you reestablish your connection with the earth and the farmer who put the grain there. When you bake, you have the opportunity to fill an artistic void. When you bake, you sow the seeds of brotherhood; what is better therapy for the soul than sitting down to a homemade pie, to share coffee and conversation with close friends and family.
—Ken Haedrich, *Country Baking*

APPLE DUMPLINGS

When we were growing up, we baked apple dumplings in a sauce made of butter, brown sugar, and cinnamon. As we tried to adapt this traditional recipe to make it healthier, we quickly discovered that the sauce was not necessary and actually hid the apple flavor behind all the sweetness.

Yield: 6 dumplings

1 cup whole wheat flour	**½ cup milk**
1 cup flour	**6 medium-sized baking apples**
2½ tsp. baking powder	**cinnamon**
½ tsp. salt	**sugar**
⅔ cup shortening	**raisins (optional)**

1. Pare and core apples. Leave whole.
2. Make pastry by sifting flours, baking powder, and salt. Cut in shortening until particles are about the size of small peas.
3. Sprinkle milk over mixture and press together lightly, working dough only enough to hold together.
4. Roll dough as for pastry and cut into 6 squares. Place an apple on each square. Fill cavity in apple with cinnamon and sugar. If desired, fill cavity lightly with raisins before adding the cinnamon and sugar. Pat pastry around the apple to cover it completely.
5. Place dumplings 1 inch apart in a greased baking pan.
6. Bake at 375° for 40-45 minutes.
7. Serve hot with milk.

WHOLE WHEAT TURNOVERS

When the children ask for a pastry treat, try these as an alternative to store-bought varieties. These turnovers also make a nice addition to a bag lunch.

Yield: 10 turnovers

Dough
3/4 cup whole wheat flour
3/4 cup flour
1 Tbsp. brown sugar
1/4 tsp. salt
1/4 cup hard margarine
1/2 cup yogurt

Filling
1/2 cup apricot preserves
1/2 cup flaked coconut
1/2 cup light raisins
1/3 cup chopped pecans

Glaze
1/2 cup sifted powdered sugar milk
1/4 tsp. vanilla

1. Stir together flours, brown sugar, and salt.
2. Cut in margarine till mixture resembles coarse crumbs.
3. Add yogurt, mixing with a fork until mixture forms a ball.
4. Divide into 10 portions. On lightly floured surface roll each portion to a 5" circle.
5. Combine preserves, coconut, raisins, and pecans. Place 2-3 tablespoons filling atop each circle. Fold one side of dough over filling. Seal edges by pressing with tines of fork.
6. Place on ungreased baking sheet. Bake at 375° for 25 minutes, or until lightly browned.
7. Cool slightly on wire rack. Drizzle with a mixture of confectioners' sugar, vanilla, and enough milk to make a drizzling consistency.

Variation:
Be creative and experiment with other filling combinations. You need about 2 cups filling for 10 turnovers.

- chopped apples
  and cinnamon
- dates
- dried apricots
- grated carrots, raisins,
  and coconut

BLACKBERRY CRUMBLE

In this crumble the fruit flavor is prominent, with just the right touch of sweetness and crunch in the topping.

Yield: Serves 6

3 cups fresh blackberries
¼ cup unsweetened
  orange juice concentrate,
  thawed
1 Tbsp. sugar

½ cup rolled oats
¼ cup whole wheat flour
2 Tbsp. brown sugar
2 Tbsp. margarine

1. Combine blackberries, orange juice, and sugar. Place in a 1-quart casserole.
2. Combine rolled oats, whole wheat flour, and brown sugar. Cut in the margarine with a pastry blender until mixture resembles coarse meal. Sprinkle over blackberry mixture.
3. Bake at 375° for 30 minutes. Serve warm.

Variation:
Use blueberries or raspberries instead of blackberries.

"Bake Until Done"

Frequently a recipe says: "Bake __ minutes," or "Bake until golden brown," or "Bake until done." What does that mean?

It is easy to set the timer for the stated minutes, but if the recipe gives a range of time, as many do, what do you do? Set the timer for the first number of minutes given and check the product.

Is it "golden brown"? While color is one indicator of doneness, it is not fail-safe. Color or brown-ness, can be more indicative of the amount of sugar or honey in a recipe. Sweeteners, especially honey or molasses, enhance the browning reaction. A golden brown color may emerge before the product is done. On the other hand, if a product contains no sugar, it will not brown very quickly. It may, in fact, be done without being "golden brown."

Testing for Doneness

1. *Yeast breads:* When tapped on the bottom of the loaf, a completely baked loaf will sound hollow (like the sound when you tap a watermelon).

2. *Quick breads and muffins:* Pierce center of product with a toothpick. If the toothpick comes out clean, the product is done.

3. *Cakes or drop cookies:* Gently press finger on center of cake and release. If the indentation disappears, the product is done.

WHOLE WHEAT COBBLER

A cobbler is an economical, simple, and delicious dessert. You can make it as rich as you like by either omitting or adding margarine. The fruit can be fresh, frozen (thawed), or canned (drained). If using a sour fruit, you may want to sprinkle additional sugar over it.

Yield: Serves 4

0-¼ cup margarine
⅓ cup whole wheat flour
½ cup flour
⅔ cup sugar
1¼ tsp. baking powder
⅔ cup milk

¼ tsp. salt
2 cups fruit—
    peaches, blueberries,
    cherries, blackberries,
    or raspberries
cinnamon sugar

1. You do not need to use any margarine in this recipe, but, if you want a more buttery cobbler, try melting a little margarine (1 Tbsp. to as much as ¼ cup) in an 8" square pan.
2. Combine flours, sugar, baking powder, milk, and salt.
3. Pour mixture on top of melted margarine, or in a greased pan if you choose not to use any margarine. Layer fruit over the batter.
4. Sprinkle with cinnamon sugar. A nutmeg sugar mixture is especially good with peaches.
5. Bake at 350° for 35-40 minutes.
6. Serve warm with milk or frozen yogurt.

We argued about this recipe. Is this a cobbler? Sarah said, "No." Mary Beth said, "Yes." As we looked at other cobbler recipes, which aren't too plentiful, we discovered there are at least two schools of thought about making cobblers.
1. *A batter is made with flour, sugar, leavening, and milk. This is poured into the baking pan first, then topped with fruit and baked. In the baking the fruit sinks down through the batter to the bottom.*
2. *The fruit and liquid, sweetened and thickened, are placed in the bottom of the pan, and sweetened biscuits are placed on top and baked.*
Regardless of the way one makes a cobbler, we do agree that fruit cobblers are great!

JAM BARS

If you have some old jams or a mixture of jams sitting in your refrigerator, this is a surprising way to transform them into a sure-to-please cookie bar.

Yield: 24 bars

1 egg
½ cup margarine
1 tsp. baking powder
1 cup whole wheat flour
1¼ cups rolled oats
¼ cup sugar
1 cup jam—apricot, blueberry,
 strawberry, or blackberry

2 Tbsp. brown sugar
1 egg beaten
2 Tbsp. margarine, softened
1 cup coconut
¼ cup slivered almonds
 or other chopped nuts

1. Combine 1 egg, ½ cup margarine, baking powder, whole wheat flour, rolled oats, and brown sugar. Press this mixture into a greased 9" x 13" pan.
2. Spread jam over this crust.
3. Combine the remaining ingredients: brown sugar, egg, 2 Tbsp. margarine, coconut, and almonds. Spread this mixture over the jam.
4. Bake at 350° for 30 minutes.

PEANUT BUTTER COOKIES

While any cookie recipe can be made with one-fourth of the flour being whole wheat, peanut butter cookies are especially good made with whole wheat flour.

This recipe comes from our grandmother, who used to bake for market. We have adapted the recipe to reflect current nutritional concerns about too much fat and too little fiber. Thus, the applesauce can replace the original shortening, and some of the flour is replaced with whole wheat flour.

Yield: 6 dozen cookies

1 cup shortening or
  applesauce
1 cup crunchy peanut butter
1 cup brown sugar
2 eggs
2 cups whole wheat flour

1½ cups flour
1 tsp. baking soda
1 tsp. baking powder
½ tsp. salt, if using a salt-free
  peanut butter

1. Cream shortening or applesauce and peanut butter.
2. Add brown sugar. Beat well.
3. Add eggs and beat until fluffy.
4. Add flours, baking soda, baking powder, and salt, if needed.
5. Chill dough for several hours.
6. Shape dough into balls 1" in diameter. Place balls on greased cookie sheet. Press flat with a fork.
7. Bake at 350° for 12-15 minutes.

Note: If you use applesauce in place of shortening, you may need to vary the amount of flour, due to the juiciness of the applesauce.

SHAGGY CARROT COOKIES

A great way to sneak carrots into an unsuspecting child!

Yield: 4-6 dozen cookies
(depending on how much cookie dough is eaten before baking!)

¾ cup shortening
½ cup sugar
½ cup brown sugar
2 eggs
1 cup whole wheat flour
1 cup flour
½ tsp. baking soda
½ tsp. baking powder

⅛ tsp. salt
2 cups rolled oats
1 cup coconut
1 cup packed grated carrots
1 cup nuts
1 cup carob or chocolate chips
1 tsp. vanilla

1. Cream together shortening and sugars.
2. Add eggs and beat well.
3. Gradually blend in flours, baking soda, baking powder, and salt.
4. Stir in rolled oats, coconut, carrots, nuts, chips, and vanilla.
5. Drop by teaspoonfuls onto a lightly greased cookie sheet.
6. Bake at 350° for 10-12 minutes.

PEPPERNUTS

As a child, I first learned about Peppernuts from an older friend who made hundreds of them every Christmas to give to her friends. She rolled out the dough and used a thimble to cut each tiny little cookie. It took hours, but her Peppernuts were all beautifully uniform. This recipe simplifies the shaping process but does not sacrifice taste.

Yield: Too numerous to count but not to eat!

1 cup honey
¼ cup margarine
1 small egg
½ tsp. cinnamon
¼ tsp. ginger
⅛ tsp. cloves
¼ tsp. cardamom

⅛ tsp. allspice
¾ tsp. baking powder
¼ tsp. baking soda
2 cups flour
2 cups whole wheat flour
¼ cup finely chopped nuts
⅓ cup hot water

1. Cream honey, margarine, and egg together.
2. Sift together all dry ingredients. Add to creamed mixture, along with nuts and water.
3. Roll dough into long, ¾" diameter sticks and freeze overnight between layers of waxed paper. The next day, slice ⅜" thick and place on greased baking sheet.
4. Bake at 400° for about 10 minutes. Peppernuts will be hard after they cool. Their spicy taste ripens if you store them in a closed container for several days. They keep for months in a closed container.

HIGH ENERGY RAISIN COOKIES

Since these cookies travel well and are so full of nutrients, they can serve as a quick meal. Try them with a glass of milk for a hasty breakfast or with raw vegetables and milk for lunch.

Yield: 1 dozen large cookies

½ cup oil
½ cup peanut butter
  (crunchy preferred)
½ cup honey
1 tsp. vanilla
½ cup soy flour
  (or instant nonfat dry milk)
¼ tsp. baking powder

½ tsp. salt
¼ tsp. baking soda
¾ cup whole wheat flour
⅓ cup wheat germ
⅓ cup unsalted sunflower seeds
1 cup rolled oats
¾-1 cup raisins
¾-1 cup dried apricots

1. Combine oil, peanut butter, honey, and vanilla until smooth and creamy.
2. Combine soy flour, baking powder, salt, baking soda, whole wheat flour, and wheat germ. Add to creamed mixture and beat well.
3. Stir in seeds and rolled oats.
4. Coarsely chop the raisins and apricots and work into the dough.
5. To form cookies, place about ⅓ cup dough on greased cookie sheet. Flatten and form into a circle.
6. Bake at 375° for about 12 minutes. Let cool on sheets for 5 minutes before moving to cooling racks.

Note:
Other dried fruits may be substituted for some of the raisins and apricots. Dates, currants, and/or prunes are good.

CHEWY GRANOLA BARS

Our husbands predict that this recipe alone will sell the cookbook. It's an all-time favorite.

Yield: 24 bars

⅓ cup brown sugar
⅔ cup crunchy peanut butter
¾ cup honey
2 Tbsp. hot water (optional)
2 tsp. vanilla
2½ cups rolled oats
1 cup whole wheat flour

¼ cup wheat germ
½ cup sunflower seeds or nuts
1 Tbsp. sesame seeds
1 cup chocolate or carob chips
½ cup raisins *or* other finely
   chopped dried fruit
½ cup coconut (optional)

1. Mix brown sugar, peanut butter, honey, water (optional), and vanilla until well blended.
2. Stir in rolled oats, whole wheat flour, wheat germ, sunflower and sesame seeds, chips, raisins, and coconut (optional).
3. Press mixture into a greased 9" x 13" pan.
4. Bake at 350° for 15 to 20 minutes, or until lightly browned. Cut into 24 bars while still warm. Cool completely before removing from pan.

BREAD-BAKING
Know Your Ingredients

FLOUR

Wheat flour provides the basic foundation of bread. It contains the highest amounts of gluten, a substance that holds air in the dough and expands like hundreds of small balloons, giving dough its elasticity and rise.

The best flour for bread-baking is a high protein flour, that is, a hard wheat flour. The protein content should be 13% or more. (Unfortunately the required "Nutrition Facts" food labels give only the grams of protein and do not give the percent of protein). The major flour manufacturers make all-purpose flour with an 11% protein content. The protein in the flour is what forms the gluten in the bread.

Whole wheat flour contains all the elements of the wheat kernel (bran, germ, and endosperm). The wheat germ and bran contain good amounts of B vitamins and fiber.

Whole wheat flour contains more natural oils than white flour and can become rancid at warm temperatures. If you plan to keep whole wheat flour longer than two months, it is best to refrigerate or freeze it.

All-purpose flour is either bleached or unbleached. We prefer unbleached flour which has the bran and wheat germ removed but has not been bleached with chemical whiteners and contains no preserving chemicals. Bleaching flour is mainly a cosmetic procedure.

LIQUID

Along with the flour, a liquid is the only other essential ingredient in bread. A variety of liquids can be used; the most common are water and milk.

Water should be medium hard with natural mineral salts which help strengthen the gluten. Soft water can produce sticky dough.

Milk adds nutritional value, helps the crust brown, makes bread smoother and softer, and extends the keeping qualities of yeast breads. Raw milk must be scalded and cooled before it is used because it contains an enzyme that interferes with yeast development. However, pasteurized milk can be used as is.

Instant nonfat dry milk is an easy, economical, and efficient way to add milk to yeast dough. You will note from the recipes that it is our preferred way. By combining the dry milk with the flour, and then using water as the liquid in the recipe, you simplify the mixing process and eliminate having to warm the milk. For recipes that call for milk, substitute ⅓ cup dry milk and 1 cup water for every cup of milk called for in the recipe.

Potato water is simply water in which peeled potatoes have been boiled. It is an old favorite addition to yeast dough. Potato water creates a moist, velvety bread. Potato water can be stored in the refrigerator for several days. Since it develops the same enzyme that is in unpasteurized milk which interferes with yeast development, be sure to scald and cool refrigerated potato water before using it in yeast breads.

Buttermilk, yogurt, and whey are good additions. They add tang, as well as the tender, light, moist texture provided by all dairy products.

Other liquids such as vegetable juices add color and wholesome flavor. Fruit juices and purees also add fresh flavors to breads. It is best to use unsweetened juices for yeast breads.

SALT

In yeast breads, salt enhances the flavor of the other ingredients. It adds structure to the dough by strengthening the gluten and preventing excessive yeast action. If your bread seems to rise quickly and crack frequently, it probably does not have any or enough salt in it. Because salt inhibits the yeast's growth during its early phases of development, it is best not to add salt to the liquid used to soften the yeast.

YEAST

Yeast is a living microscopic fungus (plant) that makes dough rise and makes bread light. Warm water reconstitutes and activates dry yeast granules. Sugar or starch feeds the activity, which releases tiny bubbles of carbon dioxide gas.

The temperature of water used to dissolve yeast is crucial. If the water is too cool, the process is slowed down. If it is too high, the yeast is killed. The best temperature is between 105°-115°. Initially it is good to use a thermometer until you become familiar with feeling the right temperature. It should feel cool enough to be comfortable but warm enough that it still registers as warm.

Heavily chlorinated tap water can interfere with yeasts' action, since yeast is a beneficial fungus and chlorine is anti-fungal.

For many who have never made bread, yeast seems unpredictable and intimidating. Through experience one learns that yeast is really quite accommodating, forgiving, and flexible.

Yeast is available in three forms: Fresh active (compressed cake), active dry, and RapidRise. We prefer—out of convenience and habit—active dry. We usually buy it in bulk by the pound. However, we have written all our recipes in terms of packages of yeast. A scant tablespoon of yeast is equal to one package of yeast.

Yeast should always be used before the expiration date printed on the package. Store yeast at a cool room temperature or in the refrigerator. To extend its life beyond the expiration date, freeze it.

FAT

Fat and shortenings tenderize crusts, add flavor, and increase loaf volume. Fat also improves crumb character and keeping quality. Breads last longer because fat slows moisture loss.

Fats include margarine, butter, shortening, and oils. Shortening and oils are 100% fat, whereas butter and margarine contain about 20% water. Oils make a richer tasting, cakier bread. Liquid oils are healthier than hydrogenated oils. Margarine and butter tend to make a flakier dough. Olive oil is especially tasty in pizza dough.

SWEETENERS

Sweeteners include brown and white sugars, honey, molasses, jams, and dried and fresh fruits. Because they are a ready source of food for the yeast, they accelerate the action of yeast.

Sweeteners also add flavor and give bread crusts a rich brown color. If your bread seems to brown too quickly on top, consider decreasing the sweetener in the recipe.

Liquid sweeteners, such as honey, molasses, and syrups, are more concentrated than granulated sweeteners and can be used in smaller amounts in breads. We discourage the use of sugar substitutes. They do not hold up when heated to the high temperatures required for baking bread and result in bitter tasting breads with unappealing textures.

EGGS

Eggs, especially the yolks, aid gluten development by increasing the stretchability of the dough without making it sticky. Eggs add flavor, color, and nutrition. They improve texture and keeping quality. We do not recommend substituting egg whites for the eggs, because, while it is a good idea health-wise, egg whites firm the end product.

OTHER

"The sky is the limit" as far as the variety of other ingredients you can add to breads: fresh, dried, canned, and frozen fruits; nuts; cheeses; spices and herbs; onions or garlic; and vegetables such as pumpkin, squash, dried tomatoes, and potatoes.

These all add flavor and texture to the dough. However, you must be careful not to inhibit the gluten from developing by too much or too many additions. Often additions are not made until after the first rising, thus allowing the gluten to develop.

"Using all the pig but its squeal" and "scraping the bottom of the barrel" are old-fashioned phrases that were modeled for us by our parents. In my kitchen hangs a New England proverb:

> Use it up
> Wear it out
> Make it do
> Do without.

We were taught good stewardship of the earth's resources. The disciples of Jesus, after feeding the multitude, gathered up the leftover fragments so "that nothing may be lost" (John 6:12). We save food leftovers. When we bake bread we use leftovers by blending them with the liquid for the bread recipe; then proceed according to the recipe directions. You may need to adjust the amount of flour you use. But the results will certainly be interesting, flavorful, and sometimes colorful. We've used leftover cooked vegetables, spaghetti with tomato sauce, beans, lentils, rice, and a variety of soups.

Index

ABOUT THE AUTHORS

We are sisters who as children had to share a room and household chores. It was our mother, Margaret Mininger Bucher, who had the vision to preserve the old water-powered grist mill that was part of our childhood homeplace in the mountains of West Virginia. She also shared with us her enjoyment of cooking, her love of trying new recipes and foods.

So it is no surprise that we both graduated from college with majors in Home Economics. Sarah continued with degrees in Early Childhood Education and in Occupational Therapy. Mary Beth received a master's in Foods and Nutrition and became a registered dietitian.

This cookbook, however, does not grow out of our formal education; instead it rises out of our experience and our love of whole grains.

Currently, Sarah lives in Mount Joy, Pennsylvania, with her husband Herb and the youngest of their three daughters. Sarah is an occupational therapist at Wernersville State Hospital where she started a "Dough-it-yourself" bread-baking therapy group.

Mary Beth is a consultant dietitian in private practice. She lives near the homeplace in West Virginia with her husband Lester who is the miller at The Old Mill. Together they also direct Mountain Retreat, a small Christian retreat center with a theme of "discovering the connection between the spiritual and the organic sources of life."